About the One Earth Books

During its nearly one hundred years of educating the public about environmental issues, the National Audubon Society has rarely achieved anything as important as reaching out to the world's young people, the voices of tomorrow. For Audubon and its 600,000 members, nothing is so crucial as ensuring that those voices speak in the future on behalf of wildlife.

Audubon reaches out to people in many ways—through its nationwide system of wildlife sanctuaries, through research vital to helping set the nation's environmental policy, through lobbying for sound conservation laws, through television documentaries and fact-based dramatic films, through *Audubon* magazine and computer software, and through ecology workshops for adults and Audubon Adventures clubs in school classrooms. Each of these is critical to reaching a large audience. And now, with the Audubon One Earth books, the environmental community can speak to the young minds in our citizenry.

Aubudon is proud to publish One Earth in cooperation with Delacorte Press. In addition to bringing new information and experiences to young readers, these books will instill in them a fundamental concern for the environment and its decline at the hands of humanity. They will also, it is hoped, stimulate an undying interest in the natural world that will empower young people, as they mature, to protect the world's natural wonders for themselves and for future generations.

We at Audubon hope you will enjoy the One Earth books and that you will find in them an inspiration for joining our earth-saving mission. Young people are the hope for our future.

> Christopher N. Palmer
> Executive Editor
> President, National Audubon
> Society Productions

ONE EARTH

SAVE OUR FORESTS

RON HIRSCHI

Photographs by Erwin and Peggy Bauer and others

National
Audubon
Society

DELACORTE PRESS/NEW YORK

For Jim

If you would like to receive more information about the National Audubon Society write to:

National Audubon Society, Membership Department
700 Broadway, New York, New York 10003

Executive Editor: Christopher N. Palmer
Special thanks to Roger DiSilvestro.

Published by
Delacorte Press
Bantam Doubleday Dell Publishing Group, Inc.
1540 Broadway
New York, New York 10036

Text copyright © 1993 by National Audubon Society
Book design by Charlotte Staub

Library of Congress Cataloging in Publication Data
Hirschi, Ron.
Save our forests / Ron Hirschi ; photographs by Erwin and Peggy Bauer and others.
p.   cm.—(One earth)
Includes index.
Summary: Discusses the characteristics and importance of different kinds of forests and the life they support.
ISBN 0-385-31076-5
0-385-31127-3 (pbk)
1. Forest ecology—Juvenile literature.   2. Forest fauna—Juvenile literature. 3. Forest flora—Juvenile literature. 4. Forest conservation—Juvenile literature. [1. Forest ecology. 2. Forest animals. 3. Forest conservation.] I. Bauer, Erwin A., ill. II. Bauer, Peggy, ill. III. Title. IV. Series: Hirschi, Ron. One earth.
QH541.5.F6H57   1993
574.5′2642—dc20   92-37385
CIP
AC
This edition is published simultaneously in Delacorte Press hardcover and paperback editions.

Manufactured in the United States of America

December 1993

10 9 8 7 6 5 4 3 2 1

MVA

Contents

ONE EARTH

Introduction

Forests are many things to many species. Their trees give you the pencil in your hand, the roof over your head, and most of your writing paper. They became this book. They are newspapers and an incredible number of other things that fill our daily needs. How we replace the trees we borrow from nature's forests is important because trees are the main structural feature of the forest. As walls and ceilings hold a house together, and flour holds a cake together, trees hold the entire forest together.

Forest trees are oxygen givers. They provide homes for bears, deer, butterflies, beetles, great gray owls, warblers, chickadees, people, and many other life forms.

They protect us from the wind, hug riverbanks, prevent floods, trap the rain, and hold on to snow, slowly releasing life-giving moisture to streams and rivers.

Even in death, forest trees protect life. They fall to the ground, nourishing the soil, providing dens for foxes, and offering meals to beetles and salamanders.

But forests are far more than just trees. Like all natural communities, they continue to exist and thrive only because of their many wonderful and varied pieces. Imagine the forest as a complicated puzzle put together over time, lots of time. All the pieces—the plants and animals living in the forest—interlock in ways we will probably never fully understand. Some forest creatures are big and fierce. Some are so small, you need a microscope to see them. Other pieces have not yet been discovered, yet play important roles in the life of the forest. Sadly, many of the pieces of our forests have already been lost forever.

In the pages ahead, you will read about endangered faces in endangered places—the many plants and animals you can help save by protecting their threatened forest homes. You will also learn about intricate balances within the many forests of North America.

You will discover that no matter where you live, you can help save and even restore forests and the wildlife dependent on them. Look through these pages, and you will see that quite a few animals are included. Many, many more could be discussed. But these species were selected to inspire you to begin your own forest-saving projects. Most of the plants and animals in this book need all the help they can get. They are in trouble. They also include indicator or representative species—plants and animals that, when helped, also end up helping lots of others because their habitat needs include the needs of other species. For example, if you help protect grizzly bear habitat, you end up protecting many square miles of forest that provides a home to elk, deer, bluebirds, owls, hawks, falcons, and other wildlife.

Think about the animals discussed in these pages, but also think about the woodland animals near your home. There are hungry birds to feed, seeds to plant, and trees to protect from destruction, as well as whole forests to restore to their former health.

While we don't expect you to save the world's forests single-handedly, you can adopt a tree for your very own, share your backyard or schoolyard with some chickadees, learn more about life within different kinds of forests, and find ways to live that help make our forests and all the Earth healthier. One Earth is all we have. It is in your hands.

Mountain Forests

When we think of North American mountains we often think of snow, glaciers, rock, ice, and wide-open spaces filled with wildflower meadows. But between the highest peaks and the lowlands where people live, there is often forest, too.

These mountain forests were never as important as they are today. In the not-too-distant past they were only one of the many homes available to endangered animals. Wildlife, especially big and fierce animals like grizzly bears, wolves, mountain lions, and wolverines, were free to roam America's lowland forests, too. But now that we have destroyed so many of the lowland forests, mountain forests are often the only places left for our rarest wildlife. Like castles in the sky, these wooded peaks have become a sacred kingdom—a last stand for the grizzly, for the wolf, and for wild forests themselves.

A walk through a mountain forest is a visual feast. While the types of trees growing at high elevation may include many you see in the lowlands, they also include some you will never see unless you hike way up high into the clouds.

Mountain hemlock, alpine firs, whitebark pine, and Rocky Mountain juniper all live best or exclusively in the high country. Many wildflowers will only grow at high elevations, too. The mixture of these flowers, shrubs, and trees *forms a distinct community*. That community changes dramatically from one side of the mountain to the other. It also changes geographically, just as lowland forests vary from one part of the country to the next.

Forests on each side of a mountain are quite different, mainly because of the varying amounts of rain or snow they receive. They also vary greatly depending on exposure to the sun, with south-facing slopes almost always being hotter and drier and sparsely covered with plants adapted to those conditions. No surprise, then, that north-facing slopes or those with greater amounts of rainfall can support lush forests with dense tangles of ferns, shrubs, and wildflowers. It is strange to think that only a few miles away from slopes covered with cactus there are often woodlands so wet that tiny frogs can lay their eggs in puddles that form in moss-draped tree branches.

Despite these differences, forests on both sides of a mountain often share one sad feature in common. Most mountain forests have been disastrously scarred by forest clearing and road building. Soil erosion from road construction and logging often tears chunks of land from these slopes. Sometimes landslides happen soon after clearing takes place, but other times severe erosion occurs slowly. For example, the stump of a tree that has just been cut down might hold on to the soil at its base for quite a few years. As the tree's roots rot with age, the soil will loosen and wash away. When the stump finally slips down the mountain, it will carry additional soil with it. Loose soil will then wash into mountain streams, destroying fish and other wildlife that depend on clean water for survival.

Fortunately, some of our national parks and wilderness areas include vast forest regions that are still intact. Here in the mountain forests of the West, you may still see grizzly bears or hear the howl of wolves. Here we may still learn ways to protect and restore other woodlands and wildlife.

Grizzly Bears

One of the largest land carnivores on Earth, the grizzly bear once roamed forests, mountains, and prairies throughout the

INDICATOR SPECIES

Coal miners used to take canaries down into mine shafts. When the birds began to have trouble breathing, the miners knew it was time to leave the mine and come up for air. In the same way, other animals in nature serve as indicators for us. These are extremely sensitive species that begin to disappear when our actions make it difficult for them to live in their natural habitat.

Grizzly bears, wolves, eagles, and other animals, such as the spotted owl, are all indicators of how well we are treating the land. When they have trouble surviving, it is an indication that all is not well.

Look at forests or small patches of woods near your home or school. You can observe many kinds of indicator species to help find out how the forest is doing. Some species will even share more with you than that!

Walk through the woods, searching for woodpecker holes in trees. The presence of woodpeckers is just one indication of forest health. Woodpeckers will be present if enough fairly large, old trees are available for feeding and for nesting. If woodpeckers can be found, you can be sure that many other hole-nesting animals will also be able to find a home.

There are many other different kinds of indicators too. Check out a field guide to lichens, for instance. Look for trees with these little plants growing on their trunks. Then keep track of a square-foot patch of lichen growth over time. (Because this is a long-term project, try to get a teacher interested so that your work is carried on year after year.) Because lichen flourishes in clean air, we can learn a lot about pollution levels in its area. In general, the greater the amount and variety of lichen, the better the air quality.

West. We don't know exactly how many there were, but many grizzly experts say there were about 100,000 prior to European settlement. The grizzlies ventured out into open country to seek a wide range of food, including plants, ground squirrels, and even bison. Before the arrival of Europeans, grizzlies had little to fear, though they were killed on occasion by Native Americans. After non-Indians moved into the West, however, the grizzly was among the very first animals to disappear.

3

How could such a large, fierce, and seemingly fearless animal vanish from most of its former living space?

There's more than one answer to this question. Grizzly bears need lots of room to roam. Their massive bodies can weigh more than a thousand pounds. It takes a lot of food to support such a large predator, and the bears can't just walk into a grocery store to buy what they need. They eat elk, deer, salmon, trout, squirrels, mountain sheep, cows, ants, beetles, moths, and other animal food. They also eat large quantities of grass, berries, and the nuts of pine and other trees. To find enough food, grizzlies range over several square miles. This home range can be entirely forested. Usually their habitat also includes meadows or prairies, such as the open country within Rocky Mountain parks like Yellowstone.

As winter approaches, grizzly bears search for a place to sleep through the coldest months. But their favorite sleeping and feeding places are almost all taken by people or domestic animals.

GRIZZLY BEAR DISTRIBUTION

Grizzly Bear Distribution 1800

Grizzly Bear Distribution 1990

At one time nearly half of our country was home to grizzly bears.
Now grizzlies live on only a fraction of our land.

Source: U.S. Department of Agriculture, Forest Service.

4

Since grizzly bears are so large and have a need for vast living spaces, they have never been as abundant as many other animals. This is a basic fact of nature; small animals and those that eat only plant life are usually far more abundant.

As a result of this phenomenon, it did not take long for people to eliminate the grizzlies within an entire state and, ultimately, throughout most of the lower 48 states of the country. They were and still are killed by people who do not want bears near their homes or where cattle and sheep graze. Remaining bear populations have become very widely scattered and separated from one another. They live mostly in refuges, primarily within Glacier and Yellowstone national parks. The land in spaces between these parks and refuges is becoming even more inhospitable than ever because of people, cattle, and sheep. Consequently, small grizzly populations are left isolated in dwindling islands of forested habitat.

Grizzly bear populations are healthier in Alaska, but the same problems occur as more and more habitat is either altered by logging or settled by people. Today, a total of about 600 to 900 survive in just four of the lower 48 states, all of which are located in the Far West. This is about 1 percent of their original population. Outside the United States, these great bears can still be found in remote mountainous areas within Europe. The grizzly reaches its highest population levels in what used to be called the Soviet Union.

Even where grizzlies are protected within parks, they are still threatened in many ways. Until very recently, for example, a legally sanctioned hunting season allowed people to shoot grizzly bears that left the borders of Glacier National Park. Many other bears are killed by trains that cross through bear habitat. Others are illegally shot in and outside of the national parks. But the greatest threat to the long-term survival of grizzly bear populations remains habitat destruction and human intolerance. There is a great deal of available land that could serve well as bear habitat, yet it is off-limits to bears for one reason or another.

This off-limits habitat covers thousands of acres in several western states, including areas such as the land around Yellowstone National Park. For the small populations of grizzlies that remain, the park has become an island. The barrier people have placed between the bears and the land surrounding the park is as great as a thousand miles of ocean. People won't make grizzly bears a high priority in our national forests. And where more and more private land is farmed, ranched, or developed for other uses, grizzlies almost always lose their homes.

Recent research warns that even the grizzly bears within Yellowstone Park are faced with extinction within the next hundred years, because they are isolated from other grizzly populations. Bears can't leave the park in search of mates and new food sources without bumping into people. Whenever the bears do come in close contact with civilization, there is a strong risk of conflict. And whenever there is a conflict, bears are almost always the losers. The death of even a single grizzly, especially when there are so few, is a great loss.

In places like Yellowstone, where an estimated 200 grizzlies still manage to survive, park officials try to help people avoid conflicts with the grizzly, especially during critical times of the year. Grizzlies will sometimes attack and even kill people to protect their little ones or their favorite feeding grounds. The park officials use "people management" to set certain places off-limits to people to make sure we don't wander too close to a mom bear and her cubs or to hungry bears just out of their winter dens. The idea is to manage human actions in hopes of eliminating the problems that sometimes arise when people unintentionally encounter a grizzly.

It's easy to see that people management is wise. No one wants to be eaten by a bear. In fact, most people want to see bears survive. Think about how this concept of managing our actions can also be used to protect other animals. Just like a grizzly, every animal has its needs, and most might attack us if we bothered their offspring or habitat. Maybe deer or squirrels wouldn't eat us, but they still need a safe home away from human disturbance. If we respect their needs in the way that people-management policies suggest, we may someday have forests filled with far more wildlife.

Unless you live near a national park, you probably don't have grizzly bears living anywhere near your home. In fact, grizzly bears may never live anywhere in your entire home state. This is even true within former grizzly bear habitat, a situation that you may want to help change.

To date, most, if not all, people working to save the grizzly from extinction are trying to protect *existing* bear populations. Some attempts are being made to help grizzlies move into land near these existing populations. This includes land alongside Yellowstone. Even in that area, they have a very hard time helping grizzlies to expand their range.

However, no one seems to be working to bring grizzly bears back to former homes such as the State of California, where the last one was killed in 1922 at Horse Corral Meadows in the mountains of Tulare County. People have, it seems, settled for a world in which bears can live only in parks. Some people are concerned, though, that the parks have become like giant zoos. They fear a world in which the only wild forest left is confined within park boundaries as surely as we confine lions and tigers behind bars.

Take a look at field guides to learn more about the ranges of grizzly bears and other large mammals. Some good field guides will show you the former range, but for the most part, only existing homeland is highlighted. This is frightening, because it suggests people are forgetting what once lived in America. In forgetting the past, we often give up hope for the future.

MOUNTAIN CHICKADEES

Many kinds of chickadees live in the forests of North America. Mountain chickadees live only in the Rockies and western coastal mountain ranges. Their voice is a little grittier than that of the black-capped chickadees you might see in your backyard. Nesting in tree cavities, they depend on woodpeckers to chip out a home for them. You can attract chickadees by placing a nesting box at the edge of even the smallest patch of trees. You can also join with other people to form trails of chickadee nest boxes that link pathways. One such route, called the Trail of Dreams, was begun by students at Wickliffe Elementary School in Ohio. To join their project, find a birdhouse book in the library, select a chickadee house plan, and build a few nesting boxes with friends or classmates. Place your chickadee house in a wooded area near a stream or river, and watch what happens next!

If you choose to work for the future of grizzly bears and other forest wildlife, yours will be one of the most difficult jobs. You can't just go downtown, apply for a grizzly-saving position, and expect to be hired tomorrow. There are no Grizzly-Bears-Are-Us shops at the mall. You can't mail-order a wild bear, a couple of wild elk herds, or a few thousand acres of mountainside. But you can learn to help the grizzly. A great start is in understanding forest ecosystems and protecting existing forests from further destruction.

Forest ecosystems include all the parts of and all the goings-on within a given wooded area. The ecosystems in which grizzly bears still live are like giant land puzzles that still contain most of the pieces we have lost in our other forests. The members within these ecosystems, like individual grizzly bears, do not think about state or national boundary lines. In fact, there are no clear lines drawn around the pieces of an ecosystem.

Forest ecosystems live and thrive because of the ways land, water, plants, and animals go on with their lives together. We can help ecosystems like those supporting grizzly populations by making sure all their pieces remain intact. One of the healthiest ecosystems in our country is the land in and around Yellowstone National Park, often called the Greater Yellowstone Ecosystem.

Yellowstone National Park, like all parks, has a boundary line that completely encircles its forests, mountains, and valleys. Many people work to protect grizzlies and other plants and animals inside the park. But others also work hard to protect land outside the park, since animals try to extend their homes into forests beyond the boundary line.

River valleys and forested mountain ranges that extend north and south hundreds of miles beyond Yellowstone were once home to the grizzly. Protecting these pieces of the entire ecosystem is not easy, but it is critical to grizzly survival and the survival of wolves and other large animals. This protection can begin by helping aspen trees, woodpeckers, bluebirds, ground squirrels, and other plants and animals in and beyond the park. Ultimately, these plants and animals are part of the grizzly's world. Simply stated, all of these lives are entwined. The larger the animal, the more land to which it is connected. If grizzlies can't find enough ground squirrels to eat or enough room to roam, they will vanish, as they have in California, Colorado, New Mexico, and most other states, as well as Mexico.

If your state once offered homes for grizzlies, maybe you could work to create a forest refuge for bears. At the same time, you could also work to make sure that other predators, such as the black bear, mountain lion, wolverine, fisher, and bobcat, do not go the way of the grizzly. These animals and others are more common than grizzlies in parts of the United States, but they are also vanishing as their habitat is altered or destroyed.

In many states, such as Louisiana and Ohio, black bears are already very rare or nearly gone. This is because of extensive forest clearing that has taken place since the earliest days of European settlement, and because of other forms of habitat destruction. It is as if forest ecosystems in Louisiana and Ohio have been torn into a thousand-piece puzzle and tossed out the window of a speeding car. Finding each piece of that shattered ecosystem puzzle is an important job many of you are already helping to accomplish.

Whitebark Pines

If you were a grizzly bear, the seeds of a whitebark pine would be as tasty as a pizza, a hot-fudge sundae, or your favorite candy bar, and as healthy as a well-balanced meal. If you had any kind of hunger for these trees, as the grizzly certainly does, you would not want to hear that many scientists consider the whitebark pine a rare and endangered species. Imagine life without your favorite snacks. Worse yet, imagine no nourishing foods to eat at all. That's pretty much what happens when any animal loses its food supply. Nobody builds new restaurants for animals.

Rocky Mountain grizzly bears eat whitebark pine seeds to fatten up in the fall, just before they enter their winter hibernation dens. At times the seeds amount to more than 60 percent of the grizzly's diet.

Fires that swept through Yellowstone and the northern Rockies in 1988 destroyed as much as 25 percent of the area's pine trees. Trees are regrowing, but it takes a whitebark pine a long time to produce cones and seeds—about a hundred years. Grizzly bears can't wait that long for a new food supply, especially when they are faced with so many other threats to their survival. And researchers say that even without the fires, seeds from whitebark pine were in great abundance only once in 10 years. To make matters worse for the trees and their dependent wildlife, disease and insect attacks threaten pine populations throughout their range.

Whitebark pine is a little-known piece of the mountain-forest ecosystem. It grows at about 8,500 feet above sea level in the Rockies and other western mountains. Its seeds are so big that the wind cannot carry them. So the whitebark pine depends on animals, especially squirrels and birds called Clark's nutcrackers, to spread its seeds to new places. Nutcrackers fly off to meadows, sometimes 15 miles or more away from pine forests, to stash a supply of seeds. Some of the seeds are eaten later, but since the birds don't always retrace their paths, the seeds that are left in hiding sprout, creating new stands of whitebark pine at the edges of high mountain meadows.

Nutcrackers are vital to the pines. Ironically, so is fire—at least the kind of natural wildfires that periodically swept through all forests at one time. For the whitebark, fires cleaned house. They burned down other kinds of trees that grew taller than they did, blocking out the sun. Fire also burned down diseased trees, reducing the number of insects and other causes of tree death. Natural fires were especially effective in helping control the devastating outbreaks of pine-bark beetles.

As soon as people began controlling forest fires, the pine community changed. Disease increased, pine-bark beetles took their toll, and taller trees of other species grew over the tops of the low-growing whitebarks. When fires did occur, they were often bigger and burned over larger areas. The human-caused Yellowstone blaze of 1988 swept through the mountains, severely upsetting the old balances between pines and the rest of the forest.

Little research is available to document all the impacts of the fires and ecological changes since 1988. But new research is helping people realize how vital the whitebark pine and its seeds have been for grizzly bears and other wildlife. Squirrels help out, stashing seeds away for the future, just as the nutcrackers do. Their hidden nuts are raided by hungry grizzlies, which eat the seeds and sometimes the squirrels, too. All participants in this natural scheme—pines, squirrels, bears, nutcrackers, and even fires—once existed together without help from people.

These ecosystem balances are never static. Nature is always changing. Forests always change, and an occasional fire is a very important part of the scheme of things. Some people say we must try to manage forests as they were once managed by nature, that we must let fire periodically sweep through and make room here and there for new pines to grow. Allowing the forest to burn is a difficult decision. But if fires are used in ways that mimic nature, burning may help save the whitebark pine, the bears, and other members of mountain-forest communities.

Although you probably do not live anywhere near a whitebark pine forest, there may be other trees in your neighborhood that are not well understood. Have you ever read a book about dogwood trees, vine maples, river birches, or pawpaws? Not much is known about these and hundreds of other trees, but you could help people learn more about them.

You could also adopt a tree for your very own, as students are doing throughout the country. Or write about your observations of trees, publishing your work in book form or in some other creative way. Always be sure to share your work with others who are trying to protect the great variety of trees in our forests too.

Elk

Few people think of elk as being in danger of extinction. Large herds roam many western mountain forests. But elk once roamed eastern and central states, including New York and Illinois, before being killed by the thousands, just as bison and mountain lions were. Like forgotten ancestors, elk rarely cross the minds of many people who live in Virginia or Wisconsin, two states where elk once lived with their predators, the wolf and mountain lion.

Even today, as abundant as they are in some places, elk are in trouble.

Consider the elk herds that have lived for centuries among the S'Klallam Indians of the Pacific Northwest. Prior to the arrival of European settlers, the S'Klallam were able to hunt elk in forests along every river valley in the northwestern corner of Washington State. But from about 1850 to 1900, when settlers arrived, elk were shot and killed, and their habitat was severely altered. Even after 1900 elk were killed just so non-Indian men could have elk teeth as ornaments for their pocket-watch chains.

Today elk face new threats. They are restricted mainly to

DRAWING ATTENTION TO OUR FORESTS

Like Gary Larson, many young artists have been drawing cartoons to call attention to environmental problems. The expression of our concerns may take many other creative forms, including the simple act of asking tough questions or of imagining what seems impossible. Maybe we could all think like Darcy Whittaker, a student in Columbus, Ohio, who imagines us restoring all of the eastern forests of the United States by pulling forth the West as if it were a giant windowshade. Darcy believes that by using the grizzly bear forests of the West, especially areas such as the Greater Yellowstone Ecosystem, as models, we could restore all the forests of our country.

Still other creative ideas offered by students measure how well we are doing in our efforts to restore individual forested areas, such as the patches of woodland near our schools. You, too, can measure forest health by using bears as an index. Although this is a fairly slow-paced kind of measurement, creating a chart and tracking bear populations as they relocate throughout the United States just might get people's attention.

Look at field guides, trying to find all the states where black bears live, as well as where grizzly bears still survive. Try to discover how much of each state is populated by bears and what areas once supported them. Then search for the forested areas that could be restored, thinking of the past, the present, and a better future for forest ecosystems.

Your bear index might be structured like a scale, ranking each forested area from 1 to 10. Perfect scores would be reserved for any area with healthy, nonthreatened populations of bears. Add sets of maps that you draw to your index. Make additional sets of wildlife index charts, showing people how other animals are doing in your state's forests. Since big and fierce animals are often the first to disappear, begin with mountain lions, bobcats, and other predators.

As a long-term goal, try to make your state a perfect 10 — a healthy area with a forest ecosystem supporting all its parts, from squirrels to great bears. Collaborate with other kids, and teachers who can help you place your work in environmental fairs for the whole community to see. Or send your work to publications, as sixth-grade student Erika Proegler has done, so that thousands of other kids can read and think about your ideas. (Publications interested in your work include IN OUR HANDS, Wickliffe School, 2405 Wickliffe Road, Columbus, Ohio 43221.)

the mountain forests of Olympic National Park. They venture down into lower elevations in far fewer valleys than before. Dams, on rivers flowing from the Olympic Mountains, block their migration routes. Logging in all valleys, new dam-construction proposals, and increased human activity all threaten elk further. In one valley alone, more than 50 percent of the elk's wintering forestland has been eliminated during clearcut logging in recent years. Unfortunately, this is a valley of great importance to the elk and to the S'Klallam people.

S'Klallam tribal members have called for the protection of elk within the valley of the Dosewallips River, citing treaties our country signed promising to protect the rights of Native Americans. In 1853 the United States government told the S'Klallam people they would always be able to hunt in their usual and accustomed places. To the S'Klallam, this means that elk and the forests used by elk will always be available to them, as in centuries past.

Biologists working for the S'Klallam are leaders in efforts to protect elk and their mountain-forest homes. These efforts are one of the many ways we hope to save wildlife and their habitat, but the task is difficult when so many people want to cut down all the forests. Maybe as we rethink how our country has treated Native Americans and their treaty rights, we will find better ways to protect resources the S'Klallam and other Indian peoples lived with, hunted, used, and respected for centuries. Maybe we can find ways to restore elk and other animals in river valleys that lead down from mountain forests throughout our country.

Wolves

Maine. New Hampshire. New York. Ohio. Wisconsin. Colorado. California. West Virginia. Wyoming. North Dakota. New Mexico. Massachusetts. The list goes on to include virtually every state. They all held populations of wolves at one time. What more can we say except that the gray wolf has vanished from essentially all its former range. Even in the small areas where wolves attempt to regain their homeland, some people either shoot them or prevent them from reestablishing a permanent home in other ways.

Where are our wolves? Why will we not allow them to return? Imagine, within the next 24 hours—from right now until tomorrow at this same time—an additional 256,000 people will be born into the world. So why can't we make room for one more wolf?

Consider the wise counsel of the Iroquois. Once, when a group of Iroquois were planning to move into a new area, they feared the presence of wolves. At first it was suggested that all the wolves be killed to make room for the new village. Realizing this was unfair, one person suggested that a member of the village be elected to represent the wolf's interests in council meetings. He or she would be a spokesperson for the wolves. It was agreed, and the move to the new village was completed. Each time a decision was made that might affect people and wolves, the wolf spokesperson was called upon. To this day, no Iroquois, nor anyone else in North America, has ever been reported killed by a wolf. In fact, the wolves and the people lived together in harmony until non-Indians began disregarding the needs of forest animals.

Now we are the ones who must decide if wolves deserve a place on our decision-making councils. Maybe it is time once again to make room for wolves. Only humans can take land away from wolves, and only humans can give it back.

Habitat conditions vary from place to place, but a pack of wolves with as many as a dozen or more individuals can live in a space of about 200 square miles. Look on a map. Search for forests of at least 20 miles by 10 miles. When you find one, you will have discovered a *potential* home for wolves. Now look for other factors: Is the forest sparsely populated by people; does it provide habitat for large hoofed animals; is it heavily crossed by roads? Answers to these questions will help determine if the area is suitable for wolves. If it is, you can help bring wolves to this special place, just as biologists and concerned citizens are trying to bring them back to Yellowstone National Park.

If past generations could land a person on the moon and create the technology of television, computers, and compact discs, then certainly your generation can put as much energy into creating a future in which forests are complete with the howl of wolves. The sound of their running feet and the thrill of their chase as they seek food for themselves and their pups can be a part of many forests once again.

Kids have already made a difference in helping wolves by adopting them as special animals for their school. Others have written letters, urging their protection or encouraging their reintroduction into former mountain forests. Maybe you could be a wolf spokesperson, too, like the Iroquois. Wouldn't it be wonderful to have people representing the wolves, the bears, and other animals of the forest each time a decision was made to cut down a tree? Many environmental groups attempt to protect the interests of these and other animals, but there are more environmental problems than there are people working to solve them.

A WOLF RETURNS

At one time Yellowstone National Park managers believed that coyotes and wolves were eating too many elk, deer, moose, and other animals in the park. They began a program of elimination, killing approximately 6,000 coyotes and 125 wolves between 1910 and 1927. But as this book was going to press, historic photos were taken of what is believed to be a wolf within Yellowstone National Park. The wolf, along with a female grizzly and her cubs, was feeding on the carcass of a bison. A coyote was also present, offering the photographers a good comparison, which helped them identify the much larger wolf. The return of the wolf is a sad reminder of past attitudes toward predators, attitudes that still linger in some minds.

But the very vision of a coyote and bears sharing a meal with a wolf is a hopeful sign that they may also share parklands with more wolves in the future.

Today there are many people who want to see wolves return to Yellowstone, and attempts are being made to reintroduce wolves from other areas. This may not be necessary if wild wolves wander into the park to establish populations on their own. But many people oppose the presence of the wolf. They say that wolves are a threat to domestic animals outside park boundaries.

Differences of opinion about wolves will continue to prevent them from returning to many areas. For now it appears that the wolves have won their own battle for a living space, and the return to Yellowstone is a great victory for wildlife and for all who have fought so hard to bring wolves back.

One of the greatest forest ecosystems on Earth, the broadleaf woodlands of the eastern United States once covered the land where most Americans now live. It is difficult to imagine just how vast, how varied, and how inspiring these forests must have been. It is also difficult to imagine how we destroyed and devastated them and their wildlife communities in such a short time. It was, as one European observer noted, as if Americans hated forests.

Chestnut, beech, walnut, oak, hickory, ash, dogwood, gum, sycamore, maple, aspen, cottonwood, elm, tupelo, basswood, locust, cherry, American holly, sassafras, persimmon, willow, and more mix together still, creating what remains of the once dominant landscape of eastern America. As if they were mannequins in the window of the biggest store on Earth, these trees seem to have many accessories—the shrubs, wildflowers, insects, birds, mammals, and amphibians that live and grow with the taller woodland plants. The mix of trees combine with one another in seemingly endless assortment, sometimes dominated by oaks, maples, or beech, but always changing in mix from one place to the next.

Forest diversity in North America reaches its peak in these eastern woodlands. They are extremely varied, even today, after so many changes. Once they were home to different varieties of life, including wolves, mountain lions, elk, and other animals now restricted mostly or entirely to western mountains. Eastern broadleaf forests were also home at one time to the single most numerous bird to ever live. Passenger pigeons flew in sky-darkening flocks that took many hours to pass by overhead. They numbered in the billions. They were all shot or killed by forest destruction. The last passenger pigeon died in Cincinnati on September 1, 1914.

Southern woodlands were home to passenger pigeons, too. The once vast bottomland forests of the Missouri and Mississippi river valleys also gave ivory-billed woodpeckers, the largest woodpeckers ever to live in our country, a place to

Eastern Broadleaf Forests and Southern Woodlands

17

live. These woodpeckers are now extinct in the United States, but a close relative may still be present in Cuban forests, though in such small numbers that little hope remains for its continued survival.

Other species hold on in limited numbers in scattered, remnant forests of the South and East. Cougars survive in Florida. Ocelots may still live in Texas. Black bears are returning to several regrown eastern forests, where bobcats have been staging comebacks, too.

The diversity of our eastern and southern forests is far greater than can be described here, but there are many ways you can get to know the forests firsthand.

Spend some time in local woodlands. Watch birds, insects, butterflies, and other animals. Search for tracks and signs of wildlife in woods near your school. Record your observations, and let others know what you discover. Then visit other, more extensive woodlands, comparing your woods with each that you explore. Why are they different? How can you help each one stay healthy? Is there a way to connect the forests to make them bigger? Can you make a pathway of trees, linking city woods with country woods? Is there a forest near your school that can be joined to a forest at another school?

There are lots of questions you can ask and lots of projects you can begin to help eastern forests. You can even plant a woodland where none exists now, restoring land that was once forested. But choose your trees carefully, selecting seeds from local trees, just as kids in Ohio and New York have been doing for two projects—one with Ohio's Nature Conservancy and one with New York City's Central Park Conservancy.

When people involved in the Ohio project could not find native tree seeds through commercial sources, they asked kids from elementary schools to go out in fall to collect acorns. Hundreds of these oak seeds were donated to be planted in former forestland that had been cleared many years ago. In time the acorns will grow into an oak woodland, the first step in restoring the land to its former health. People have also been working in New York, planting native trees, shrubs, and flowers in Central Park in an attempt to restore a forest landscape in the middle of our largest city.

If you want to restore forests by planting seeds, look in a library for the U.S. Department of Agriculture Handbook Number 450, SEEDS OF WOODY PLANTS IN THE UNITED STATES. It will help you select and grow seeds from trees. You might even start a wild-tree nursery in your school. Start off with oaks, which are easy to grow, easy to find, and valuable to most wildlife. They are also one of the most characteristic trees of eastern broadleaf forests. Simply gather some acorns in fall, plant them about 8 or 12 inches apart, then cover them with an inch of firmly packed soil. You can plant seedbeds of up to 35 acorns per square foot, imitating natural tree growth. Cover your seedbed with leaves or straw, then cover that with something like chickenwire or hardware cloth. Remove the leaves in spring, and allow the seedlings to grow for a year. The next fall you should cover this area again with a new layer of leaves to protect the little trees from the winter cold. You can transplant yearling oaks to an area once forested and in need of your restoring work. Maybe you can find a place along a stream or river that has been abused. There are lots of places like that in eastern broadleaf forests and throughout our country. They will continue to look gross and disgusting until we take care of our forests once again.

Imagine all the places you have seen on your way to school that look like they were bulldozed or forgotten. Think of how many kids there are in your school. If 350 of you each planted 35 acorns this fall, and you wrote to other schools to ask if they wanted some of your acorn seedlings, you might just start a forest so big that rare and endangered species would feel welcome to return. Read Jean Giono's THE MAN

WHO PLANTED TREES for an inspiring look into the possibilities of forest restoration.

Warblers

Some people mistake certain warblers for wild canaries. While warblers live in tropical forests during our winter, they try to find homes in northern forests, especially eastern broadleaf forests, each spring. They come in lots of species, the way new clothes come in lots of styles. They are all a slightly different color, and each sings its own wonderful song.

Warblers are like the musicians of the forest. Actually, their name refers to the beautiful, warbling songs they sing. Maybe their songs can be used to help save them. Go out into the forest in spring. Listen for their songs. Record them. Create a warbler dance to celebrate their return in spring. You could even dance to the sound of their recorded song. Make bird costumes. Hold a contest for the best-dressed warbler in your school. This dance should be held to help make others aware that warblers need us to protect their forest homelands, especially during the winter months, when the birds are not here in our country.

Write to kids in Central and South America, discovering what can be done to help keep the warblers' winter homes in tropical forests safe, too. A good place to start is the MONTEVERDE CONSERVATION LEAGUE, Apartado 10165-1000, San José, Costa Rica. The league helps to protect and also to purchase rain forests. Maybe you could start your own warbler conservation league, helping to protect and even purchase eastern broadleaf forests.

Black Bears

Black bears certainly outnumber their relative the grizzly. About 200,000 are thought to live in the lower 48 states, and there are substantial populations in Alaska and Canada.

WILL POWERS AND THE TRAIL OF DREAMS

Will Powers loved the environment. He worked to create a path from his school down to a nearby river. But he did not live long enough to see how wonderful that path had become. Will died when he was struck by a car in the spring of 1991. To remember Will, his classmates, other members of his community, and people all across the country created a memorial fund in Will's name to continue his work and concerns.

Today, the Trail of Dreams is a national project of forest restoration, stream cleanup, and pathway creation extending from Will's hometown to the home of an endangered animal he and his friends wanted to help. Their idea was to create a trail of trees from their school in Columbus, Ohio, all the way to the Rocky Mountains of Montana. As kind of a wolf highway, their trail would be a restoration of forested lands all the way along the Missouri, Mississippi, and Ohio rivers. The ultimate goal of their project is to bring back endangered species and to have fun, too; after all, the trail is a great place to build hiking and bike-riding paths.

Nationally, many people have begun to restore small pieces of forestland and riverbank woodlands — all because some kids at Will's school cared enough to dream about restoring our land to its former health. The Trail of Dreams is being built step by step in communities that keep in touch through the WILL POWERS MEMORIAL FUND, Wickliffe School, 2405 Wickliffe Road, Columbus, Ohio 43221. Write to the fund for more information, or begin a trail of your own, contacting other groups, such as RAILS-TO-TRAILS CONSERVANCY, 1400 16th Street NW, Suite 300, Washington, DC 20036.

More adaptable than the grizzly, black bears can live fairly close to humans, but they are still in trouble in many woodlands.

Smaller than the grizzly, a large black bear can weigh about 500 pounds. They eat lots of berries, grass, insects, and some meat. They also like to eat the inner bark of trees, a habit that gets them in trouble with people who grow trees for lumber.

A black bear can strip the bark from a young Douglas fir, sometimes killing the tree. This makes the tree growers angry, because it threatens their livelihood, but there are lots of things the tree growers do that threaten bears and other wildlife, too. For instance, many tree growers have managed to eliminate all but one kind of tree in vast areas of woodland.

When a forest loses all but one or two tree species, the variety of species within the forest decreases dramatically. That diversity is the very stuff that keeps the forests healthy and thriving over time.

Loss of diversity and forest health begins when a commercial tree company cuts down maples, alders, oaks, ash, aspen, and cottonwood trees and replaces them with one species, such as Douglas fir or some kind of fast-growing pine. Commercial companies plant these few kinds of trees

FOREST FRAGMENTATION

Putting the forest back together again is a monumental job, but someone has to do it. We broke the forest, so we have to fix it.

Basically, the people who came before us chopped up the woodlands of America into many tiny pieces. This is true in every corner of the country where forests grow.

You can get a good idea of which forests are healthy by finding those in which bears or other large mammals still survive. Since these larger forest animals need more space than smaller wildlife, the forest habitat supporting them will generally be in better condition. That almost always means that the woodlands haven't been quite as segmented.

Two tools will help in your research: a map of where large forest animals still live, and a map of existing forest fragments that need "fixing."

A good field guide will help you locate areas where black bears still live. You will probably be surprised to find that many black bears are living quite close to civilization, possibly near your own home.

Next, find an aerial photograph of a forested area near your home or school. Usually a city or county engineering office will give you a copy of its planning photographs that cover five to ten square miles. Draw a map of the forests you find within the areas covered by the aerial photographs. Your map will often be covered with spots, like a dalmation. The spots and dots of forest don't really

connect in many parts of our country. There are blobs where a big patch of forest still thrives. But there are also big chunks of land where cornfields have been planted, cities have been built, and other forest clearing has taken place.

Your mapping can help the future of forests and forest wildlife. Begin visiting the forest fragments you discover on the photographs. Begin making surveys of wildlife in woodlands of different sizes. Try to get others interested in the woodlands near your home and school. And try to find ways to connect the dots. That will be the hardest job of all, since virtually no one in America has ever tried to do that.

because of their quick growth and because the lumber markets demand the kind of wood that comes from them. They grow them like farm crops, cutting down the trees when they are tall enough to sell as lumber or other wood products. In the process, they rob forests of their diversity and wildlife of their homes.

Diversity is the untidy stuff of life. Healthy forests demand it. In fact, an ecosystem's health suffers without it. Diversity in the forest community simply means that each member is different and each has a unique role in keeping the balances within the community.

So many of our environmental problems result from the loss of diversity within a particular ecosystem. Take away critical pieces of the forest puzzle, and we may never be able to put it all back together again. Maybe black bears don't think about their homes in this way, but since we are aware of the need to protect each of the forest's varied pieces, maybe we should think for the sake of the bears.

If you were a bear, you might view the forest a little differently than most humans do. As a bear, you might consider squirrels tasty treats. Maybe you'd like to eat a couple of mushrooms, too, and some seeds from a tree. You might even wonder how all those pieces—the squirrel, the mushroom, and the seeds—were connected to the forest. Actually, it is as if the forest were a giant pizza for bears. As outrageous as it may seem, even a squirrel's poop is a critical ingredient in that monstrous and edible woodland.

Consider this. A squirrel hops down from a tree. Looks around. Sees a nice juicy mushroom amid a cluster of mushrooms where beetles, ants, and spiders make their home. The squirrel munches a couple of mushrooms for breakfast, then runs down a freeway of logs, jumps up in the branches, scampers up a tree trunk, down another, then runs from a hungry bear and into a clearing in the woods. There the squirrel poops.

Hidden from our view, inside the squirrel's droppings, are the seedlike spores of the mushrooms. Without knowing about its importance to the forest's future, the squirrel has just planted a mushroom, far from where the mushroom first grew. Out in a clearing, the seeds of trees fall from high branches. Some are even carried here by a bear, then left behind in its droppings.

The real magic of all this poop business takes place as the tree seedlings and the new mushrooms begin to grow. Squirrel poop becomes the cheese topping, mushrooms the favorite additions to the woodland pizza. And the trees grow much better in their company. Tiny rootlike threads, called *mycelia*, which the mushrooms use to gather their food from soil, wrap around and into the roots of the trees. The trees band together, as if joining hands beneath the soil. Each helps the other get more nourishment; some plants will not even grow without this partnership.

Now, if only tree growers thought of the forest as if it were a giant pizza. Maybe they would let the bears chew bark on trees more often. After all, the bears were chewing on trees long before Europeans arrived in North America— when the forests were vast, tall, and healthy, when they were diverse. For the bears, the diversity meant they had lots of options. They did not have to eat just bark, just squirrels, or just mushrooms. It is only when we force them to live in a forest with only one or two kinds of trees that bears become a problem for the commercial tree grower.

We took pieces of the forest away, little by little. We can bring back each piece little by little. It will take some time, but what better thing to do with our time than to help restore forests to their former health?

Gray Foxes

Gray foxes are tree climbers. Although they nap in the branches, they make their secret homes down deep in the

24

dark cavities within old oak trees. They are much more at home in the woods than is their more familiar relative the red fox.

Gray foxes eat many pieces of the forest, from persimmons to beechnuts. But they are only one of many animals that depend on the seeds, berries, fruits, and nuts produced each year by broadleaf trees or the shrubs that grow beneath their canopy on the forest floor. In the rich and varied eastern woodlands, seed supplies are incredibly abundant. This is true where wild tangles grow free. It is also true where forest fragments are allowed to grow right in our midst, within large cities, in suburban woods, and in your backyard.

Wild cherry, blackberry, acorns, grapes, hazelnuts, and even poison ivy berries are valuable gray fox food. More than a hundred different birds and other animals join the fox in the woodland diner where blackberries are available. The list of blackberry-eating wildlife includes chipmunks, cardinals, orioles, grouse, song sparrows, raccoons, rabbits, towhees, bears, and people, too. But people often try to clean up this tangle of blackberry vine, especially where the forest and city meet.

Small woodlands, particularly those near or within cities, are tidied up as if they were bedrooms and the city parks department were your mom or dad. As more and more homes are built in or near forests, the woods are assaulted by people who seem to have a need to clean things up. Little do the tidy people know that the forest thrives best when allowed to toss its leaves, seeds, and berries in every possible direction.

The next time you are part of a tree-planting project, think about the needs of gray foxes and other blackberry consumers. Add some wild shrubs to your wild garden. Each tree you plant is only one small part of the larger forest. Work to convince others that tangles of berry vines and a large variety of trees and shrubs will make a healthier and more meaningful forest. Planting shrubs that easily become tangled may be untidy, but these plants are the mark of a true forest and make more comfortable homes for the gray fox and other wildlife.

If you live in a neighborhood where gardens are so tidy that animals no longer find homes there, try to talk your parents and neighbors into creating wildlife gardens. Think like a fox. Try to plant whatever it needs. Look for places where you might climb into the branches to hide, where you could find enough berries for lunch and dinner, or where you could crawl into the snug warmth of an old oak to raise your pups. Thinking like a fox and acting like a wildland gardener, try to plant the missing pieces of your own fox woods.

American Chestnuts

Once one of the most important and numerous native trees east of the Mississippi River, the American chestnut is now endangered.

Often when we think of endangered species, we think only of birds or mammals. But plants such as the chestnut may deserve even more attention than animals, since they offer homes and food to a wide variety of wild creatures. Once gone, trees and other plants leave a gap in our ability to restore the forest, especially when the disappearance involves a tree as important as the chestnut.

The ecologist Gordon Orians says there are always at least two causes for a loss in nature. One is the *proximate cause*, a cause we can usually see and even stop from bringing about any short-term, irreversible damages. The other, called the *ultimate* cause, often lies buried in the past. Actually, the ultimate cause may not be just one thing at all. It may be a series of things that results in a negative impact over time on our environment. Because ultimate causes are so difficult to identify, they are often more difficult to correct.

The proximate cause of the American chestnut's decline is

FOREST COMMUNITY DIVERSITY

Take a closer look at forests of the United States. General types of forest, such as eastern broadleaf, are actual communities consisting of trees and other plants. The dominant or most abundant trees in any given place define the forest community, as shown on this map of the original woodlands of Ohio. If you wish to restore an entire forest or just plant a single tree, learn which are the dominant members of your local forest community, then use them as starting species for your efforts.

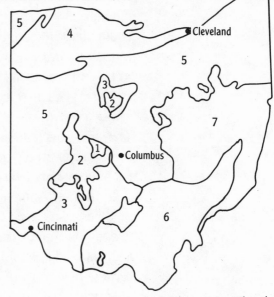

To see how this works, review this list of major plant communities in Ohio and the map on this page.

(1) Prairie. These grasslands were dominated by big bluestem, switch grass, and Indian grass. This is true tall-grass prairie, with some grasses growing to over eight feet in height.

(2) Savannah. This is a mixture of oak and hickory forest, with tall-grass prairie openings.

(3) Oak-hickory forest.

(4) Elm-ash forest.

(5) Beech-maple forest.

(6) Mixed forest of high diversity. The mixture includes maple, buckeye, beech, tulip trees, oak, and linden.

(7) Oak forest.

Now pretend for a moment that you live near Columbus, Ohio. Your first choice of trees to plant within this community should be number 5, beech-maple forest. But remember that while beech and maple may dominate this forest, many other trees — including oak, hickory, cottonwood, and walnut — are a part of this plant community, too.

One of the best ways to discover more about plant and animal communities associated with your region is to read historical accounts of the forests of your area and to visit protected natural areas and large arboretums. (For example, the Dawes Arboretum near Newark, Ohio, maintains an intact old forest with towering red oaks, large walnuts, and other native species.)

a disease called chestnut blight. The disease was introduced into our country from Asia in about 1900. The blight has taken a deadly toll. In fact, it is now tough to find even a single chestnut in many eastern states.

But the blight was not completely responsible for the death

and disappearance of chestnuts from our forests. They have also disappeared because we changed the eastern forests so dramatically. It is not possible to know which of many reasons is ultimately responsible for the lack of chestnuts and many other trees in these woodlands.

Eastern forests, like others, evolved over many thousands of years. Trees grew together in a community of many species. Those forests were healthy and acted more or less like a city. They had ways to treat disease, for example. While no doctors come to call on a sick chestnut, other members of the forest community may tend to it.

If an insect starts eating a tree, a healthy forest has lots of other insects, chickadees, warblers, and woodpeckers to swoop down and eat the attacker. Before too much damage is done, predators of these would-be pests are taken care of, because the forest community more or less takes care of itself over time. A healthy forest also contains lots of varieties of the same kind of tree. When chestnut trees were widespread and numerous, some of them were naturally more resistant to diseases. Because there was a greater variety of chestnut trees as a whole, some of them survived, passed on that ability to survive, and kept the forest healthy.

We may never know whether the chestnut trees could have been saved if we had been able to protect a greater number of them prior to the arrival of chestnut blight. We do know that thousands of acres of chestnuts were logged and burned prior to that time. Some of those lost trees could have held the ability to resist the blight or other diseases. That is a great risk we take today in clearing so many acres of forest—in doing so, we eliminate valuable diversity.

When we cut down almost all the forests of the East during the past few centuries, we destroyed critical balances. Today we know that the diversity within those forests cannot be replaced. This is the concern we have for the future of tropical forests and all remaining woodlands within our country.

When we destroy vast acres of any kind of woodland, the most feared loss is diversity. Without it there are no equivalent doctors and hospitals to care for nature's sick.

Whenever we clear away a variety of trees from the forest, we take away the very pieces of the forest that can help it survive. In that way people may often be the ultimate cause of tree deaths that lead to the endangerment of species. We may even be the ultimate cause of the extinction of the chestnut.

Cats

Cougars, ocelots, margays, bobcats, lynx, jaguars, and jaguarundis are all native to North America, primarily to the southern and eastern forests. Only the lynx does not wander into the Deep South. But few of these cats can still be found anywhere in our forests.

Also known as mountain lion, puma, and panther, cougars may weigh more than 200 pounds, though males are considerably larger than females. Like bears and wolves, they need lots of space. As a result of their need to roam, cougars are almost gone in the entire eastern United States.

A small population of cougars survives in southern Florida. Known as the Florida panther, the big cats are being helped by people trying to protect their dwindling habitat. Roads, houses, and other land uses continually encroach upon the borders of wetlands and dry forests where the cats manage to survive.

As the largest of American cats, the jaguar has nearly vanished in our country already. The last one known to be in California, for example, was killed near Palm Springs more than a hundred years ago.

Ocelots are rare golden cats with black-bordered spots. They climb trees and catch birds far more skillfully than your pet cat. But they can't survive without complete protection

CELEBRATING LOSS . . .

Each year the town of Hinckley, Ohio, holds a Buzzard Festival — a special day celebrating its history with food and crafts. Most people look at it as a day to get together and just have fun.

Many would be surprised to learn that the annual festivities actually commemorate the "Great Hinckley Hunt" of December 24, 1818. On that day in history the townspeople went out and killed 17 wolves, 21 bears, 300 deer, and uncounted wild turkeys, foxes, and raccoons. Buzzards (turkey vultures) gathered to feed on the dead. Today buzzards still come to Hinckley, but there are no wolves, no bears, and few of the many other animals killed that day.

Wouldn't it be wonderful to incorporate the restoration of wildlife into the festivities at Hinckley and in other towns throughout the nation? Wouldn't it be wonderful to help bring wolves, bears, and other large mammals back to our forests?

from hunting, trapping, and the pet trade that kidnaps them from their homes. Ocelots are in high demand by people who like to take wild animals from the forest to tame. An estimated 80 to 120 survive in Texas. They remain very much in danger of extinction in our country and in Mexico.

Margays, weighing only about five pounds, are even more rare than ocelots and have been seen in the United States only in the wilds of west Texas. They are in grave danger of extinction.

Like all other animals, margays and ocelots do not think much about international borders. But they would benefit greatly if the United States and Mexico decided that together they should protect endangered cats and their forest homes. More of these wild cats remain in Mexican forests than in our country. They would enjoy a future in those southern woodlands beyond our borders, and might even travel into the United States more often if you and your friends adopted their needs.

Learn what you can about Mexican forests. Read more about margays and ocelots, as well as other animals in forests to our south. Also try to find ways to restore forests, especially along the streams of Texas, Louisiana, and Arkansas, as well as in Mexico. Write to wildlife agencies in those places to encourage them to reintroduce ocelots to forests, since these cats can be successfully reestablished if enough habitat remains available.

Search for students in Mexico, Costa Rica, and other countries who will help with your cause to save the margay, ocelot, and other cats. Maybe you will be the first person to start a student exchange dedicated to protecting wild cats throughout all of the Americas. You might even be the one to save wild cats from extinction. Ask your librarian for information on pen pals in Latin American countries, or write to INTERNATIONAL YOUTH SERVICES, PB 125, SF-20101, Turku, Finland, and ask for pen-pal information.

Red-cockaded Woodpeckers

The endangered red-cockaded woodpecker suffers extensive habitat loss in southeastern forests managed exclusively for pine-lumber production. Like most woodpeckers and lots of other wildlife, the red-cockaded needs old trees. These birds nest in 80- to 100-year-old pines, but commercial pine forests are often cut down when the trees are younger than 40 years. The entire forest is removed during logging, leaving few if any old trees and snags (dead and dying trees). A new crop of trees is planted and cut again while still too young to support the woodpeckers.

On land administered by the U.S. government, which is actually public land, forest managers are required by the Endangered Species Act to protect pine forests for the red-cockaded woodpecker. This is making a difference in some forests, but the forest managers must be reminded of their responsibility often and by lots of people. Since others who manufacture wood products try to persuade them to cut as much wood for lumber as possible, our wildlife needs your voice. Without it, lumber interests will be the only ones heard, and the woodpeckers will vanish forever.

Red Wolves

The endangered red wolf once roamed woodlands and open meadows from Texas to Florida, possibly ranging as far north as Lake Michigan. Weighing up to 65 pounds, these wolves are smaller than gray or timber wolves. They have recently been reintroduced into the wilds of North Carolina and Mississippi. But controversy surrounds the question of whether or not they still survive in the wild in east Texas and in regions bordering Louisiana and Oklahoma. In fact, some people question if the red wolf is a true species, separate from other wolves of our country.

It is not just red wolves' color that distinguishes them from other wolves. Size also helps separate them from gray wolves. Regardless of whether they are considered a separate species, these wild dogs are definitely the only wolves that manage to hold on, though just barely, to existence in the southeastern forests.

Imagine if all the flowers vanished from our yards. We'd all notice they were missing. Yet when wolves, cougars, bears, wolverines, fishers, and other large mammals disappear, we tend not to notice, because they are not as visible as the flowers just outside our windows. We may even think that life can go on without these species.

But we are wrong. When we lose wolves, we may not lose a vital link in a food chain that humans depend on for survival. But we do lose something. All of us lose yet another piece of the forest—a piece that may very well be the critical one holding all the others together.

Ancient Forests and Northern Woodlands

When Europeans first came to America, they met a wall of trees so tall and wide that people actually were able to make homes in the stumps of single fallen trees. A band of trees stretched across the northeastern and northwestern states, as well as within vast areas around the Great Lakes. But these ancient forests of pine, fir, cedar, hemlock, and spruce are now reduced to a small fraction of their former size.

The ancient forests of the eastern United States are essentially a memory, even though much of the Northeast is covered with forest and contains the most heavily forested state in the nation, based on percentage of total area (Maine). Fortunately, though, a few ancient forests remain on the Pacific coast, despite repeated attempts in the past and present to destroy them all.

There are few places on Earth where so many plants grow in such quantity as in the ancient forests of the Pacific North-

32

ANCIENT FORESTS THROUGHOUT THE AGES

Ancient Forests in 1620

Ancient Forests in 1850

Ancient Forests in 1990

We are quick to call for protection of tropical forests. But it is not possible to understand the future of forests in other countries with-out recognizing our own destructive past. It is also critical to protect, restore, and reestablish woodlands in our own country while we try to help people in tropical places from making the same mistakes we made in the United States.

(Courtesy National Audubon Society Adopt-a-Forest, Washington State Office, P.O. Box 462, Olympia, Washington 98507.)

west. Yet this region has suffered tremendous devastation. For example, only 10 percent of the Pacific Northwest's ancient forests remain standing today; many of them are lush, temperate rain forests, the last to be reached by modern forest industries. All others were cut down soon after America was settled by Europeans.

Giant cedar trees of the Pacific Northwest once dominated the rainy woodlands along the Pacific coast. These trees can grow 60 feet or more around and were the natural economic base for people who lived in harmony with these forests for thousands of years. Cedar trees were a part of the wildlife community, and they were used by Northwest Coast Indians in relative moderation to craft beautiful homes, canoes, bowls, boxes, paddles, and even clothing woven from the soft inner lining of the massive tree's bark. Cedar trees are still one of the most impressive trees in the forests of this region, but fewer of them exist since the chain saw entered the woods.

33

The Douglas fir tree is perhaps the tallest tree in the world, towering more than 300 feet high in some forests. But because these trees are also among the most highly prized lumber "products," they are now being commercially grown and cut down before they can stand any taller than 60 to 100 feet high.

But trees like the Douglas fir are far more than lumber products. And unless we begin to think of them as making more of an important contribution to our lives as trees than as furnishings, chances are good that remaining ancient forests, still home to 300-foot-high fir trees, will vanish for all time. It happened to the vast ancient forests of Maine, New York, Pennsylvania, Michigan, and Ohio, and it is happening

OUR ANCIENT FORESTS, GRANDEST ON EARTH

Still standing in a forest, waiting for you to discover them, giant Douglas firs and enormous cedars tower as high as a football field is long and spread wider than many buildings are wide. Our ancient forests here in the United States grow taller trees and include greater quantities of plant matter than any forest on Earth. Size-wise, we have some of the grandest prizes on the planet growing in our midst.

If you could scoop up all the plants growing in one acre within these forests and take them back home with you to study, you might be surprised at how much stuff you would need to pack away. If you managed to pick up every tree, shrub, wildflower, fern, lichen, and trailing bit of moss,

along with all the other vegetation in an acre of Pacific Northwest ancient forest, the combined weight might reach about 400 tons. This compares with less than 200 tons of plant matter in the same amount of space within the most luxuriant tropical rain forest you can find anywhere on Earth.

Often it is the tiny plants on the forest floor that catch our eye. And though they may not live as long as the towering giants above them, these beautiful flowers tell a story of the critical links within the ancient woods. Consider the life of many orchids. They grow and flower in spring or summer within shaded groves of old-forest trees. But they will not grow without other plants they have come to depend on for survival. Most or-

chids are linked, inseparably, with mushrooms that also grow in the damp, shaded woodlands. Their roots unite beneath the forest floor in deep, rich soil that takes many years to develop. The mushroom is then attached to the orchid's root system, helping the wild-flower absorb nutrients. So dependent is it on this helping hand, the orchid cannot live in isolation. But all partners in this relationship are dependent — the mushrooms also attach to tree roots, helping even the oldest, tallest tree to grow. The trees, in turn, offer shade needed by the mushrooms. The orchids add a splash of color to the forest floor, giving us one more small but beautiful reason to protect the forest and its diverse occupants.

right now in Oregon, California, Washington, Idaho, Montana, and Alaska, where ancient trees are cut to make products that could just as easily be made from smaller trees.

You can help make sure our remaining ancient forests do not die.

Although we have already cleared and changed much of the forests in the eastern states, scattered remnants of original forest do remain in northern regions. Only in large, intact, and ancient woodlands will you find a complete forest. This may come as a surprise to you, especially if you have wandered through the beauty of an Adirondack woodland or walked the trails of any of Maine's vast forests. These are wonderful places, but they are missing many pieces lost long ago when we destroyed the ancient woodlands and when we repeatedly cut down the forests that replaced them. Trees may have grown back, but a forest is far more than new trees.

When we allow the remaining few ancient forests to grow older still, we protect the rarest of the rare, the most threatened species of forest wildlife. We may also be saving pieces of our forest legacy, providing clues to help younger forests recover from past abuses.

Northern Spotted Owls

No single animal in recent years has drawn our attention to the need for forest protection more than the northern spotted owl.

As more and more of the ancient forests are cut down in the western homeland of the owl, fewer and fewer living spaces are available. Biologists studying these owls issued warnings that too much forest had been cut. The owls were not only losing their homes, they were losing their chance to survive. Finally the owls were declared a threatened species. Now minimal amounts of forest are being set aside to try to protect them. But there were warnings from Native Americans concerning the loss of the owl even before this recent one.

The Yakima Indian people have lived in the Northwest amid ancient forests and spotted owls for many centuries. Their land includes a part of the owl's traditional range, which extends along the Pacific Northwest rim of forestland. The Yakimas have always thought that when owls leave the forest, the end will be near. They believe the owl is a messenger telling us that when we protect the forest, the owl will be saved, and when we protect the owl, we will all be saved. The Yakima's belief says much about the way in which all of nature is connected.

The forest is certainly the only home that northern spotted owls know. But not just any forest will do. These owls need deep, shaded woods, where very little light can enter. They need forests where ancient trees tower high into the sky, offering homes to bats, flying squirrels, and even relatives of mice that live high in the branches of our oldest woodlands. These small animals lead lives of their own and fall prey to other wildlife, but for now they are especially important as the food spotted owls need most.

For nesting, the owls need big trees with broken limbs, a rotten spot with a gaping hole, or a top twisted by the wind. These old and still standing trees give owls safe, dark cavities in which to raise their young. Without these old trees, spotted owls will die.

These old trees are incredibly valuable to Japanese wood merchants, American timber-industry officials, and Hong Kong interior decorators. Anyone with an eye for the rare and unique beauty of finished wood wants the old trees cut down, milled into lumber, planed smooth, and sold to build walls, floors, or desktops. When a single tree brings several thousand dollars, owls have little chance. Owls have no bank accounts. They can't buy the trees they live in by applying for a loan. They can only depend on you and others who value all the rare and uniquely beautiful inhabitants of the forest to make sure that their homes are not cut down.

We have saved the owl temporarily by stopping at the very last moment. Most people agree that the remaining ancient forests where spotted owls live would last no longer than five years if we continued to ignore the owls' needs and cut down the rest of the big trees at the pace set by the timber industry. Pacific Northwest forests are being cut faster than the rain forests of Brazil. Fortunately for the owls and for all forest dwellers dependent on old trees, people are now trying to think of ways to save the forests and still make sure that loggers will always have jobs, too.

To sustain forests over time and protect rare wildlife, as well as the oldest of our forests, the future calls for new plans that incorporate ecological ways of thinking. Those include complete protection for the remaining few ancient forests, an idea that does not get a lot of support in many lumbering areas. People believe that jobs are being lost because of the spotted owl. But the jobs lost in lumbering areas have actually been declining for several years, not because of protection of the owl. Jobs have declined in the timber industry for other reasons, especially because of mechanization in mills and in the woods where the trees are first cut down. Modern equipment can do the work of many people who once dragged trees from the woods, hauled them to transfer points, and cut them into lumber.

Jobs have also been lost because many timber companies have failed to manage forestland for the future. That is especially obvious in the East, where virtually no ancient forests stand today. It is becoming more and more obvious to anyone who has seen the miles and miles of clearcut forest on private, state, and federal lands in the West.

In our society we always seem to wait until the owl is threatened, the grizzlies are almost gone, or the big trees are only a memory before we act. Maybe we need to rethink our relationship with the forests. But how do we do that?

STREAMS OF LIFE
Trickles of water that become a stream flow from the mossy ground beneath towering trees. Once forests are cut and cleared away, these tiny streams die because the moisture sheltered by the tall, ancient trees evaporates into the sky.

One place to start is where the damage was first done. Not only on the west coast of America, where the last big trees survive, but on the east coast, where forests are just beginning to reestablish former conditions after centuries of our presence. In fact, some students in Maine have already started a search for the biggest trees in the woods near their school. Mr. Jim Moulton's students in Bowdoinham, Maine, are looking for ancient trees, the biggest of each kind.

Maybe you can do the same, challenging other kids in schools within your state to see who can find and protect the biggest and oldest pine, oak, fir, cedar, beech, or elm. You may, like Amanda Sodergren, find an ash tree that measures 132 inches around. Or you might find a tree larger than the 192-inch eastern white pine discovered by Chad Roy or the 160-inch oak found by Robert Craig. See if you can find the biggest, the most ancient trees in your neighborhood, town, or state. Call attention to these special trees, the grandparents of the forest. Maybe you won't find a spotted owl in your search, but you will certainly find a way to show people how special our forests are.

Pacific Yews

People often ask why we should bother to save or protect the many plants growing in the forest. This is especially true of the ones we don't seem to have a demand for in our everyday life. Smaller trees that don't stretch very far into the sky or grow in great numbers have even been labeled "of no economic importance" in books meant to educate scientists who manage forestlands. Often these trees are unknown, at least to those who do not value the forest for its own sake or to those who do not understand the complex interrelationships in the woodlands.

The Pacific yew is one of those ignored trees that grow in the Pacific Northwest. Timber companies cleared thousands

BASEBALL, TREES, AND A HOME RUN FOREST

Some students, including kids at Our Lady of Peace School in Columbus, Ohio, are calling attention to the needs of trees and forests by working with sports stars. They also create tree cards like those picturing your favorite baseball, football, or hockey players.

Maybe you could get in touch with some of your favorites in college or professional sports, asking if they would be a spokesperson for endangered trees and animals that need forests to survive. We will never know who is willing to help us save our forests unless we ask. And some baseball players may never know where their favorite bat came from unless you let them know about the forests that grow ash and hickory trees.

Violins, violas, canoes, oars, sculptures, guitars, and many other wonderful things came from trees in the oldest of forests. Track down the origins of some specialized wood instruments, and you may find other sources of help in saving forests.

of acres of forest, selling only the lumber of firs, hemlocks, and cedar trees. For more than a century they burned the remaining forest, encouraging the regrowth of only one or two kinds of trees. They tried very hard and have been very successful in turning diverse forests into tree farms. Unfortunately, no one cared enough to pull yew trees from burning piles of *slash* (the waste piles where limbs, gnarled stumps, twisted old trees, or small saplings with no commercial value are discarded). Thousands, probably millions of yew trees were destroyed in this manner. Forgotten. Never replanted. Suddenly all this has changed, though. Scientists believe that the Pacific yew may be one of the cancer cures for which they have been looking.

Admired and used for centuries by Native American woodworkers, the yew is sought by pharmaceutical companies for a substance called taxol. Taxol will be used to help treat the more than 1 million new cases of cancer in the United States every year. But there is not enough taxol to go around. We have already eliminated yew trees from many forests. Many of these trees, especially the largest, grow best in ancient forests—but these forests have not been managed well by the forest industry. Realizing the value of yews, the forest companies are quickly trying to plant new trees in hopes of growing enough to supply the demand for taxol.

These efforts may not be enough. It takes 2,000 to 4,000 yew trees to produce just one kilogram of taxol. And the trees must be cut down before the bark needed for this cancer drug can be obtained. Since it can take several decades for a yew tree to grow 10 feet high, it will take a hundred or more years to replenish future crops of taxol-producing trees.

It is nice to think that we could just go out and plant some trees to restore forests. But as you can see in the case of the yew trees, it isn't always that easy. If you wanted to grow a forest for spotted owls, chances are that it would take anywhere from 100 to 300 years to create ideal conditions for just one pair of owls. And your tree-planting efforts for these owls would have to cover a thousand or more acres.

Protecting the small amount of ancient forest that remains becomes more critical when we realize how difficult it is to re-create those old woodlands. Nevertheless, it is important to do both—protect the old and plant the new. Fortunately, we have not destroyed all yew trees, so seed sources are still available. But what else might we lose if we allow more of the rare old forests to fall?

Murray Birches

Only one Murray birch tree is known to survive. Recently discovered in a northern Michigan forest, this single tree is being protected by researchers from the Center for Plant Conservation. Write to the center at P. O. Box 299, St. Louis, Missouri, 63166-0299, to find out how you can help save rare trees like the Murray birch.

Researchers at the center have been trying to let us know about problems facing other rare and endangered plants, too. In Hawaii, for instance, a single wild specimen of the palm, *Pritchardia munroii*, grows on the island of Molokai. All states have plants that vanish almost without any notice. Each state keeps lists of these endangered plants. Maybe you could adopt some of the rarest of the rare forest plants, helping to restore them to the wild. It would be a terrible loss if more plants joined the list of 200 native plants in Hawaii that have already disappeared for all time.

Think about raising awareness of rare plants by conducting a plant inventory in your area, calling attention to the trees that are disappearing from your block, your town, or your county. Raise funds to adopt rare plants, and sponsor ongoing efforts at the Center for Plant Conservation. To find out more about plants that are endangered according to U.S. laws, write to the FEDERAL WILDLIFE PERMIT OFFICE, U.S. Fish and Wildlife Service, Washington, DC 20240. Contact your local or state natural resource agency for a listing of endangered, rare, and threatened plants protected by law in your area.

Do not be surprised if you discover that little is being done to protect rare and endangered forest plants. Some states have no funds for biologists to survey, let alone monitor, the loss of even the rarest plants. Often, rare-plant locations are plotted on maps and information is gathered to locate areas needing protection. But the truth in our country is revealed in the list of losses that occur every day as we lose endangered plants during logging, land clearing, and road building. No one is watching out for the plants. It is up to you to help change that in the future.

Lynx

Like mountain lions, grizzly bears, wolves, and wolverines, lynx need lots of space to survive.

FISHERS
Not really a fish-eating animal, fishers are large weasels that live in old-growth or ancient forests. They wander widely and are generally more rare than spotted owls. In many of our national forests, their last remaining habitat is being destroyed without any consideration for their future.

SNOWSHOE HARES
The lynx walks on extra-wide feet. The snowshoe hare falls prey to this efficient predator. But the hare often escapes the lynx. Changing coats to match the season, the hare is brown in summer and snow white in winter. Like other small mammals, hares that do become food for predators are a critical link in food chains. How many steps in the food chain can you trace from the ingredients in your daily food? How many are linked in some way to the forest?

Look at their ears and their oversize, snowshoelike feet. If you were a lynx, you could probably hear a mouse scampering through undergrowth from several yards away. You could pad over to it across the deepest snow, barefoot. Your eyes, your ears, and every muscle would help you adapt to the forest world. But if you were a lynx, you would also be wearing a very valuable fur coat, one that is highly demanded by people for its fashion appeal and warmth.

Trapped for fur and driven farther into the most remote wilderness areas by logging and road building, lynx are believed to be living in New England, the Adirondacks of New York, and the northern Rocky Mountains. But we do not know for sure the limits of their range either in the East or in western forests.

You would think, after all the television specials about wildlife, all the books, and all the recent interest, that we would know a lot about where most animals live in America. Surprisingly, we know very little, since not very many people go out into the woods to look for animals unless they are searching for something to shoot, trap, or, occasionally, photograph. And there are often very few scientists hired to do surveys of wildlife, as well as very little funding to aid environmental organizations in their efforts to protect animals. For example, the entire state of Montana employs just one biologist to try to keep track of all the nonhunted wildlife in our fourth-largest state. The timber industry has more money to spend on one single advertising campaign than most environmental organizations spend for an entire year's efforts.

You can change all this by joining local efforts to survey forests or by starting such efforts in your school. What better way to learn about forests, wildlife, and the ways to protect them than by actually getting out into the woods? Put this book down for a while and take a hike. Maybe you won't actually discover a lynx, but you might find the tracks of a bobcat, its slightly smaller relative.

Get a field guide to animal tracks to help you identify signs and footprints. Make castings of tracks with plaster of paris. Look for tracks on the forest floor, spending as much time as possible along muddy streambanks or other soft ground. Or scrape away small areas along well-worn animal trails, and return to see what walks where you have cleared a track plot. Come back once a month to see how animal use in the area changes through the seasons and through the year. And remember, many animals, especially predators like wild cats, are nocturnal. Visit your forest by day to see what has been walking in your footprints by night.

Report your findings to wildlife agencies or to conservation groups such as the Audubon Society. Often they do surveys in attempts to protect local woodlands. Your discoveries will help their efforts. Your concern will also help lead others out into the real classroom; wouldn't it be great to spend some of your school year in the forest instead of learning about it from a distance?

Tree Voles

If you were a tree vole, awakened from an afternoon nap, and you looked to the ground, your view of the forest floor could be more than a hundred feet beneath your whiskers and nose. These small mammals spend their entire life high in the canopies of Douglas fir forests in Oregon and redwoods in northern California. They rarely touch the ground.

Like views from an office tower, the scene from the treetops is spectacular. The wind almost always blows. Leaves dance. But since the Douglas fir is a conifer tree, its leaves are narrow little needles—not the broad, flat leaves you might collect in the fall. They're tough, too. Since Douglas firs are evergreens, these needles remain hooked to the trees all year long. That's probably why tree voles choose to live in fir trees— the needles are available to them through every season.

SAVE OUR SALAMANDERS, SAVE OUR FORESTS

Where have all the salamanders gone?

Maybe you don't live near woods where wolves howl, grizzly bears roam free, or elk bugle in the crisp night air. But chances are good, even if you live in the middle of the city, that salamanders live in the woods near your home or school. Chances are also good that no one knows where the salamanders hide. It is up to you to find them.

Salamanders have adapted to a woodland way of life. They can be found where moisture offers them suitable habitat, dampening their skin and providing a place where they can find food. They always have to be a bit wet, but they don't necessarily need water. Just a damp spot under a log, stone, or tangle of twigs and fallen leaves. Fallen trees, stumps, and old rotting logs are favorite salamander hiding places.

But salamanders are disappearing. Scientists believe their disappearance may be due to global warming, acid rain, or forest destruction. It is more likely they suffer from a combination of these impacts. Global warming reduces moisture in some salamander woods, acid rain harms their eggs and bodies, while forest clearing takes their homes away.

Your searches can help identify where salamanders still survive in the wild. They are one of the best early warning systems we have to signal trouble for our forests. Where you find them, things may be more or less all right. Where they have vanished, though, we need to worry. And if they return to once vacant woodlands, there is hope that other forest creatures will also return. Find some salamanders today, and you can help lead the way to reintroduce larger and rare wildlife tomorrow.

Tree voles eat the needle edges as if nibbling little cobs of corn. They bite away the untasty tubelike structure in the middle that carries resin through the leaf. Then they eat what is left, a thin piece of greenery no bigger than a couple of your eyelashes.

It's a small world in the treetops where voles hide away. They build tunnels with twigs, gluing them together with the discarded resin tubes. Like little castles in the sky, the tunnels run from nesting chamber to resting places high in the branches. But like the homes of all animals dependent on big old trees, these castles often crash to the ground. The vole's world is becoming smaller still as forests are cleared and distances between canopy living places become greater and greater.

No vole freeways connect patches of woodland so these little mouse relatives can recolonize once their forest homes are destroyed. No widespread public attention is paid when they disappear. And with a limited range within the Pacific Northwest ancient forests, the voles will become extinct unless the remaining old trees are protected. Among the creatures who will miss their presence, should they vanish, is one of their only predators, the rare northern spotted owl.

Marbled Murrelets

One of the most surprising animals to appear in forests of any kind, the marbled murrelet is very much like a duck. Closely related to puffins, these birds live most of their lives out at sea. But they fly inland during a critical time of year, the season of birth.

They search for the biggest, oldest trees they can find and make nests on moss-draped branches, in old woodpecker cavities, or in broken treetops. The trouble is, fewer and fewer big trees are left for murrelet nesting places in areas such as Olympic National Forest. The U.S. Forest Service manages this and our other national forests, where it has become the world's largest builder of roads. Since 1940 it has cut more than 360,000 miles of road through public forests that belong to you and your friends. This is enough roadway to circle the Earth almost 15 times. The roads help loggers get to the ancient forests, which they are cutting at a rate of 2,000 acres per week.

Forest Service roads do not help murrelets find their way home.

The farthest inland a murrelet has ever been observed nesting is about 25 miles from the ocean. This means that old forests in lowland areas near the sea need protection as much as high-elevation woodlands farther from the sea. As with other animal protection, forest habitat needs to be available over as wide a range of geographic locations as possible. This ensures enough living places for all animals that need it.

Only a handful of murrelet nesting sites have been discovered. All we really know is that murrelets need the ocean for feeding and big trees for nesting. We don't know how many trees or what kinds. We don't know how close their nests can be to one another. We don't know if they can nest near eagles, great blue herons, or owls. Nor do we know what tree species they prefer for nesting, whether they will nest near people, or how close they will nest to roads, logging activity, or recent clearings.

If you live in potential murrelet nesting areas, you can help learn more about the birds and their needs by taking part in ongoing murrelet censuses. Contact the Audubon Society near you or your state wildlife agency to find out about audiotapes that teach you to listen for the murrelet's distinctive voice. Maybe you will hear murrelets fly in from the sea as they search for a nesting place next spring. If so, you may be able to save them and their woodland nesting sites by letting people know about your discoveries.

Goshawks

As a school project, ask your teacher to find an aerial photo of your community or one near you that includes forestland. Looking at this photo, try to find a place to nest, feed your young, and sleep at night, imagining all the while you get to fly free as a goshawk in search of a new home.

If you have trouble finding an aerial photo, get in touch with a university library, the U.S. Geological Survey, or NASA. City and county planning or engineering offices will also help you, since they often have easily copied photographs you can use as a blueprint to trace your new goshawk homeland. If you have trouble thinking like a goshawk, try to find a person who knows a lot about birds and who will agree to lead your class on a field trip to find goshawk and other inhabitants of old forests.

Although smaller than an eagle, a goshawk is a pretty good-sized hawk. Its wings are short and rounded like those of its relatives the Cooper's and sharpshinned hawks. Its tail is long and acts like a rudder as the goshawk sweeps through the trees in pursuit of its prey.

Swift and fierce, goshawks need big trees and large patches of forest to survive. Each nesting pair requires about five square miles of woodland, with some open land mixed in. This nesting area must include 300 acres or more of essentially undisturbed forest. Especially intolerant of people, goshawks need isolated forests free of logging and other human activities.

An individual goshawk looking around for a spot to live does not search as we would. That is why an aerial view of the world will help you think like one of these birds. Looking down on the tops of trees, a goshawk sees something like a swirl of green clouds. Its forest view is a kind of mosaic pattern, swaying in the breeze. If there are too many openings in that cloud of green forest, the goshawk flies on. Experience and instinct combine to help it search for the best hunting place. If trees are too young and short (for a goshawk anything under about a hundred feet high is considered short), the bird knows it can't find enough food. It searches until it discovers a large enough forest with tall enough trees, if one can be found at all. Can you find a goshawk home near your own?

Rivers and Trees

Ecologist Jim Lichatowich says that a river has at least two major parts. He calls one the river of water, the other the river of stone. By studying the relationship between rivers and the hillsides and valleys they cross, he creates an important image to help us understand long-term changes.

It takes centuries to wash soil, rock, and entire mountain-

BLACK-CAPPED CHICKADEES
Walk along a wooded stream in winter. Stop. Whistle softly. Chances are good that a chickadee will investigate, wondering who you are and what you are doing in its woods. Watch the chickadees as they move away from where you stand. They seem to pick at nothing, pecking at the tips of twigs. Like many other small birds, they are consuming insects that would otherwise swarm in thick clouds. Friendly bug patrol. Doing harm to no one, the chickadee continues to search for its insect food as we continue to offer them a home.

sides to the sea, but you can see the results of river actions almost anywhere in our country. Rain and snow fall. Streams form. Water rushes downhill. With it go little stone pieces of the mountainside.

Prior to European settlement, our rivers and streams were in a very different balance with the land. Trees grew on valley sides and on steep mountain slopes. The trees helped hold on to the stones, protecting soil and hanging tight to quite a bit of the landscape. That all changed dramatically when we cut the trees and gouged roads and clearings from the hills. Severe erosion washed more and more stones into streams.

The simplest way to see what happened in the past is to walk along a stream throughout the year and witness how it changes. Sadly, many of our streams run dry at some point. The river of water is completely replaced by a river of stone. In fact, thousands of miles of streams in our country are now buried beneath that river of stone because we did not pay attention to the relationship between the water, the stones, and the trees that hold all the pieces together.

Rivers, stones, soil, and all the vegetation in a river valley combine to form what are known as watersheds. Watersheds act like huge sponges filled with living parts. Trees are an important component of watersheds because they absorb and direct water flow, as well as keep the water free from silt and soil. Because there are fewer trees in many watersheds than there once were, we have lost a sense of how the valley worked in years past. The streams remaining near your home probably don't act as they used to. They will be normal only when forests are restored. For now, it is critical to protect remaining trees, especially along the immediate riverbank. Once the river of stone that Jim Lichatowich talks about becomes dominant in a valley, the water often runs only underground, and streams actually become buried for all time. Out of sight, the streams and their values are lost forever.

Even in the rainy Pacific Northwest, streams have been buried beneath stones. The removal of trees from steep hillsides is responsible here, as well. When left standing, trees and the forest soil regulate the flow of water into streams, while their roots hold on to the streambanks and hillsides. Streams often do not recover from large-scale clearings like those in most commercial forestland, even if the clearings are replanted with trees. In fact, studies have shown that it can take many years to recover from the erosion caused by logging. In Oregon some streams have taken more than fifty years to wash away the stones and gravel added when landslides fell into the rivers!

Battles rage in the Pacific Northwest forests where many years have gone by since people first recognized the importance of trees in watersheds. On the one hand, timber owners usually want to cut all the trees in a watershed right down to the river edge. On the other hand, stream ecologists try to protect as many riverbank trees as possible. Jim Lichatowich's river observations point to one of the clearest solutions. He says we should step back and take a close look at balances between rivers and trees. Take only enough trees so that balances are not upset between water flow, stones slipping off the mountainside, and the fish and wildlife of the river. But politicians, not ecologists, write the regulations.

In virtually every state, laws allow people to destroy rivers. New regulations such as those in Pacific Northwest forests generally favor timber industries, not rivers. Erosion is allowed to continue, essentially unchecked. If we changed these laws to reflect the balances in nature, we could revolutionize our relationship with the entire forest world. We could establish regulations that protect the natural laws, such as those operating between a stream and its watershed. With this approach, we could force industries to prove beyond a reasonable doubt that any logging, clearing, or potential polluting activities will not harm the stream. Sadly, as it stands now, people do not have to prove that their actions are harmful. The destruction of our forests and streams continues. Nowhere is more protection from that destruction needed than along the immediate river edge.

The habitat along a streambank is usually referred to as *riparian* habitat. It would be tough to draw a line with a felt-tipped pen away from the edge of a river or stream to define clearly the zone where water and land interact. But it is the area along a river with a strong connection to the stream itself where willows, cottonwoods, and other water-tolerant vegetation grow best. Trees hug riverbanks, creating a strong and vital bond between water and land. Cut the riverbank trees, and the soil erodes almost immediately into the stream. But riverbank trees are far more than just erosion controllers. They offer homes to more animals than any other forest habitat. Pathways for birds and mammals, the riverbank trees are like freeway connections, providing a safe route of travel as long as the ribbon of trees along the stream remains intact. No clear separation can be made between where the river begins and where the forest is on its own ground. Joined by stones, roots, water, fish, and herons, the riparian habitat is a unique and interrelated living place for you to get to know and to protect.

Try to replant trees or prevent trampling along streambanks. Willow, aspen, cottonwood, cedar, and other native trees live near water, and all can be planted to restore streambanks. But, as in protecting all forests, it is always best to prevent damage before it happens.

Salmon

It has taken many years for people finally to realize that fish and trees are intimately connected, just as trees and the air we breathe are connected. Trees bring life to salmon. Trees help keep rivers clean. They help water flow. Their roots hold soil as if they were clenched fingers grabbing on to the hillsides so they won't wash too quickly into streams. This is especially important where salmon lay their tiny eggs. The eggs and baby fish also benefit from branches that hang over streams, sheltering them from weather extremes. Tree leaves that fall in the water are also valuable food; fish eat the insects that eat the leaves that grow on the trees that live in the forest along the stream.

There are several kinds of salmon, many with names that speak of their long association with Native Americans. Chinook grow to more than a hundred pounds and swim out into the ocean after spending a part of their early life in streams. Coho, pink, chum, sockeye, and Atlantic salmon may be smaller, but they each have the same basic life history.

Salmon begin life as tiny eggs dug into river gravel by their mother. She swims in from an adult life in the sea and spawns with a male; then both parents die. This cycle is completed in streams where the parent fish were born two or more years before. Baby salmon survive to hatching if the forest surrounding the stream is healthy. Where too many trees have been cut and stripped from hillsides, rain and snowmelt wash silt into the streams, burying and smothering the eggs. Silt covering the thin skin surrounding the egg can prevent the exchange of oxygen with passing water. Then the baby salmon dies.

Where forests are healthy, old trees also contribute to the quality of water in salmon streams. Old trees fall into the water, giving fish a place to hide from predators or to rest on their journey upstream and downstream. Since so many other fish also rely on trees for shelter, you can help stream life no matter where you live by adopting a streambank. If salmon are present, you can protect them by making sure that trees are present on the edge of their stream. Darters, striped bass, smallmouth bass, trout, and other fish will also benefit from this measure. If trees have been cut along your stream, you will be helping greatly to improve water quality by restoring native vegetation. Plant a tree, grow a fish!

Bald Eagles

Did you know that it is illegal to kill an eagle, but perfectly legal in most cases to destroy the eagle's home? While this doesn't make a lot of sense, it is a truth that lies at the heart of almost all wildlife problems in our country. We may punish people who kill rare animals, but we hesitate to act or ignore those who cut down their homes.

A noted eagle expert recently stated that the future of this bird depends mainly on the availability of trees—big trees— for nesting. It is that simple. The trees growing along rivers are often the ones eagles select because much of their food, especially while they are away from ocean coasts, is gathered along rivers and streams. But many of these trees are routinely cut down or cleared during logging, for home sites, or for other purposes.

One way you can help eagles is to learn where they nest or spend the winter, adopting these places as if they were your own home. Contact local wildlife agencies or Audubon members to find out all you can about the ways nesting sites are being protected. Ask for information about eagle censuses. Take part in these counts, especially those conducted during the winter, when eagles are more likely to visit your area. (They travel away from nesting areas and can spend the winter in places with no nesting populations.) Make maps indicating the trees they like to sit in, since they will often hang around for a while in winter as they search for new breeding grounds. You may even discover a nesting tree never known before. But finding nesting trees is just the first step in helping eagles survive.

Once they are found, eagles can be watched from a distance throughout the nesting season. Sometimes this is the only way we can protect wild animals. As more and more people move into eagle nesting habitat, it becomes more likely that some of you will actually live quite close to these majestic birds. If you don't, you could get in touch with people who do live near eagles to lend your support to their protective efforts. This is critical, since people still shoot eagles as surely as they cut down their homes.

Even if you live far from eagle nesting areas, you can try

Join National Audubon's efforts to save ancient forests by enrolling in the ADOPT-A-FOREST PROGRAM.

Send your name and address to the NATIONAL AUDUBON SOCIETY, Washington State Office, P.O. Box 462, Olympia, Washington 98507. Ask about the adopt-a-forest project, and find out how you can help. This successful effort has been under way since 1988 and includes field studies and true protection of our last ancient rain forests.

Also contact Audubon in these areas to help protect ancient forests of California, Oregon, and Montana:

National Audubon Society
P.O. Box 3499
Eugene, Oregon 97403

National Audubon Society
209 North Clinton
Walla Walla, Washington, 99362
(to help in eastern Oregon and Washington)

National Audubon Society
3420 North Old Stage Road
Mt. Shasta, California 96067

National Audubon Society
HCR 69
Polebridge, Montana 59928

to teach others about the beauty and majesty of these, our national birds. We must make their needs known to enough people so their long-term survival is ensured. People must learn that trees are for eagles, if our national symbol is to fly forever in our skies.

Cottonwoods

Cottonwoods are one of the most widespread trees in our country. But cottonwood forests are not even considered forests by many people. This is rather strange when you consider that these forests are some of the most extensive ever to exist in North America. They once lined riverbanks in a winding ribbon of valuable woodland from the east coast to the west. Where they still exist, cottonwoods are home to eagles, owls, falcons, warblers, orioles, and many other birds.

Once, cottonwoods formed an almost unbroken chain of narrow woodland from the Rocky Mountains to the eastern border of the Great Plains. They snaked down from the mountains, growing along the banks of rivers. Like a long chain of daisies, they spread a thin line of dazzling color as fall turned their broad leaves golden. Cottonwoods seem to have been spared destruction while so many of our other forests have suffered. Since they grow quickly in the wet riverside habitat, they quickly restore themselves to cleared places.

If you have a chance to plant trees, certainly think about cottonwoods. Find a streambank in need of restoration. You might be able to connect your line of cottonwoods with those planted by other concerned people. Together you could build a trail of trees that provides animals with a pathway while protecting streambanks, too. You could help restore the forests of the past.

Trees growing in your town, city, or backyard are part of the forest in almost every corner of the country. Parks, gardens, and the trees that line highways may not be home to bears and wolves, but the trees you see every day on your way to school could be home to many more animals if you start thinking of them as woodlands and act to help add the missing pieces.

If we restore native forest plants within our cities, we can help link communities together in a new way by creating pathways of woodland. We can also provide a great and natural pathway that connects rural forests with those within town. This can help create a more livable city environment while restoring and enlarging forests all around where you live.

Chances are good that deep forests and ancient woodlands once stood where your home, school, and shopping malls now stand. The birds that sing from today's trees are the same type as those that sang in former woodlands. Squirrels and insects, too. Often, scattered trees actually make it possible for these and other animals to get from one woodland to the next. Each tree acts like a stepping-stone. Collectively, they form a path of trees that bridges the gap across spaces that were once densely forested.

You can help city woods and your own backyard forest take on more of the features of wilder woods. You can also help the wild woods farther from your home by making sure the trees in your neighborhood aren't cut down to build more places to shop or park cars. If buildings must go up, encourage the builders to leave open spaces that save the trees, calling attention to vanishing woodlands through letter-writing campaigns, calls to city officials, and contact with news media.

Try to find natural, fairly wild woods as close as possible to your smaller or more completely urban woodland, too. Go out and visit the wilder woods and take notes, photograph

City Woods and Backyard Trees

BATS

Does your city have a wooded park? Is there a small patch of trees near your school? Contact your local parks and recreation office to find out if you can place a bat house in these small city woodlands. First do some research on how many mosquitoes are eaten every summer by bats. Chances are good that you will get lots of help with your project once you dazzle people with the statistics you gather.

features you enjoy, and study how the tangles and wildflowers add to the forest habitat. Think like an architect dedicated to creating forests instead of buildings. On paper or with three-dimensional materials, design ideal forests, using the wild habitat as a model. Try to bring the natural woodland back into the city by planting wildflowers, bordering or replacing your lawn with shrubs. Replant native trees throughout your city with the help of others. Reseed bare ground, working to mimic what you see out in the forest.

Your forest restorations will take many years, but you can see results and test success each season. Take notes in spring to see how many kinds of birds, butterflies, and other animals are using your woods. Keep records of when birds first arrive in spring, holding contests to see who spots the first of each species. The more kinds of mammals you see and the more birds you hear, the more likely your woods are taking on wild characteristics. If you hear a great many kinds of birds, chances are good that your trees are serving their purpose, giving birds a freeway route to a larger forest where they will ultimately nest.

One of the biggest problems facing forests throughout our country is the loss of large, intact woodlands. Forests continually shrink. Spaces between them become wider. Woodlands once connected to one another are fragmented. They become islands.

Any way you can think of that connects woods to one another will be a great help. No one has ever found a way to do this successfully on a large scale, so your efforts to create a forest bridge might well mean that your forest-saving efforts will be one of the most significant ecological discoveries of modern times. Everyone to this day has worked hard to deforest. It is up to you to reforest, reconnecting woodlands to one another like old friends.

Art Wolfe

ANCIENT FORESTS AND NORTHERN WOODLANDS

Northern spotted owl

Cottonwood trees

Sockeye salmon

Lynx

Douglas fir

Redwood forest

Evergreens

Giant sequoias

White-tailed deer in cypress forest

Redheaded woodpecker

Monarch butterflies

Rufous hummingbird

Pine mushroom

Oyster mushroom

Red columbine

RAIN FORESTS

Diverse rain forest vegetation

Woodpeckers

We drove the ivory-billed woodpecker to extinction, cutting down too much of its forests. It is too late to save it now, but we could learn from this mistake and work to save other woodpeckers, many of which live in our backyards. Each has its own habitat needs, but woodpeckers also make homes for lots of other animals. Master builders and architects of the bird world, they'll construct homes for chickadees, squirrels, bats, owls, and other wildlife. Just give them a tree home, and they will turn it into a thriving wildlife city.

Now that ivory-bills are gone, pileated woodpeckers are the largest North American woodpecker. They need about a hundred acres for nesting and at least a dozen old trees about 20 inches or more around—big enough for the crow-size woodpecker to excavate a nesting cavity. They need more than just one big tree, since they will also use a hole they've chipped out of another tree for resting or sleeping. These big trees also provide food, and the bigger the tree, the more food tucked in branches, crevices, chipped bark, and broken limbs. Insects like to hide and burrow into the soft and decaying spaces in these ancient trees. Pileated woodpeckers love to eat them.

Snags are another important woodpecker habitat requirement. Snags are the hotels and motels of the forest. Some people despise snags, and the very word paints a picture of what they are—dead and dying, rotten old trees. Maybe people are afraid of the old trees falling on their head. This is a concern for those who do work in forests. But when was the last time you heard someone complain about a tree falling on his or her head?

If you were a pileated, hairy, downy, redheaded, or other woodpecker, the snags of the forest would appeal to you as much as a bakery or chocolate shop. A snag's soft deadwood allows woodpeckers to easily chip away in search of insect

LAWN CHEMICALS

Is your city one of the places in the country with little flags waving on lawns, warning kids and pets to stay off because of chemical application? Do a little research to discover what kinds of chemicals are being applied. Walk local streams, and see if the chemical warning flags are floating down toward the sea. Then start a campaign to find better ways to treat the land beneath our feet. Conduct a bird-nesting survey in communities with and without chemical applications. Where are all the birds? Will they be able to read the warnings on the lawn-chemical flags?

dinners. But snags disappear faster than any other feature of our forests because people have always tried to manage forests, cleaning and tidying up the woods. And wherever trees are grown for lumber or paper, individual trees are cut down long before they can grow old, become snags, and disappear as a woodpecker drills for food and a home. That is why city and backyard trees are so attractive to many woodpeckers. We seem willing to let the trees grow older in cities and small towns.

Winter is a great time to go on a woodpecker safari. Even in the busiest and largest cities, the downy woodpecker can be found then. Follow it as it pokes at branches or pecks at loose bark. Chances are good it is flying around the trees with a group of other birds. They all hang out together during the cold months, keeping close for many reasons. They help one another find food, calling as if to invite others to a newfound feast of bugs. They also stay close to one another to help keep predators away. Downy woodpeckers, chickadees, nuthatches, and lots of other small birds band together and screech at hawks or owls, often scaring them away. They even mob hawks, swooping at would-be attackers with a strength gained in numbers.

You and your forest-saving friends can also gain strength by joining together to help woodpeckers. If we band together to protect big trees, woodpeckers will spend time in our forests. And the homes they make for themselves will eventually become homes for other animals, especially those that can't build a home for themselves.

If you live near some woods with a few big trees, you can be a woodpecker surrogate—a kind of replacement or temporary woodpecker.

Build a few birdhouses, just as a woodpecker would do, excavating small holes for chickadees, bluebirds, swallows, martins, and other wildlife. Scatter the bird homes throughout the forest. In time the houses you make will be used. Once the forest habitat recovers, the temporary houses you build

CAN ART MAKE A DIFFERENCE?
Think about creating art exhibits for your local parks department. Urge the department to hold an art contest, and to place winning paintings in community-park centers or at the entry point for a local wooded park. Some kids are placing bulletin boards along park trails, carefully mounting artwork and poetry beneath protective covers. Celebrate the beauty of nature while helping others search the parks for the colors, designs, and patterns you see and recreate in your drawings.

will no longer be needed. Real woodpeckers will move in and take over the work you started. They'll be glad to replace you, and your thanks will include the sounds of these wild carpenters chipping homes in snags, tall trees, and the branches of your forest.

Hummingbirds and Butterflies

Hummingbirds and butterflies sip nectar from flowers, just like bees. They help pollinate plants as they search for food in blossom after blossom. Like gardeners in the wild, hummingbirds help ensure that seeds grow into flowers in our forests and meadows.

In England, where most large mammals of the forest were driven to extinction many years ago, lots of butterflies are now in trouble. Some are already extinct, and we can expect the same to happen in our country unless we stop the usual business of forest destruction. People in England have responded to the declines by planting flowers, shrubs, and trees known to attract butterflies. Their hope is to reverse the trend that has placed 80 percent of resident butterflies on a path of decline in major regions throughout their homeland.

Butterfly gardens are also being planted in the United States. Maybe you can design some gardens with butterflies in mind, too, sneaking in a few habitat features needed by other wildlife that may not have such popular appeal.

If you live in the western United States, rufous hummingbirds are common during spring migration. They will nest here, too, building a tiny cup-shaped nest in coniferous forests or wooded areas near gardens. They sip nectar from native plants such as gooseberry, currant, fireweed, manzanita, paintbrush, penstemon, salmonberry, and honeysuckle (try this one yourself for a taste of natural sweetness). The rufous hummingbird spends its winters in Mexico.

If you live in the eastern United States, the ruby-throated hummingbird will visit your bird feeder or nonnative garden

FEEDER TRAILS
Sunflowers placed in small feeders along wooded pathways help people to see birds at close range while they eat. Chickadees, nuthatches, downy woodpeckers, cardinals, finches, and other birds will visit feeders. Try to talk your teacher or after-school activity director into creating and maintaining a local feeder trail. Chances are good that the more people you can get to enjoy the birds, the more people will help protect the homes of these and other wildlife species.

plants. Many people stop right there, completely satisfied that their yards have attracted hummingbirds. You can really help out by more fully re-creating natural habitat. Plant wild gardens, selecting from some of the more than 30 plants that ruby-throats help pollinate. These include trumpet vine, cardinal flower, scarlet lobelia, fly honeysuckle, trumpet honeysuckle, royal catchfly, fire pink, small red morning-glory, buckeye trees, bee-balm, pinkroot, and scarlet hibiscus. Plant these in ways that reflect how they grow in wild woods you visit, and you will also be helping restore habitat for lots of other wildlife.

Woodland butterflies you can help include emperors that feed as caterpillars on hackberry. Tortoiseshells, angelwings, ladies, and peacock butterflies exist in varied habitats, including woodlands. They feed on several kinds of trees. Hairstreaks are little butterflies that feed on trees or shrubs. The Araxes skipper lives in open woodlands in the South; its caterpillars feed on Arizona oak trees.

You can discover more about butterflies, observing them in the wild and conducting field searches near your school. Go first to survey the area, looking for the butterflies, caterpillars, and good habitat. Look in the library for a field guide such as the AUDUBON SOCIETY FIELD GUIDE TO BUTTERFLIES, written by R. M. Pyle. He has done a great deal to help save vanishing butterflies and the woodlands they need to survive. Also contact the XERCES SOCIETY, 10 SW Ash Street, Portland, Oregon 97204. Its mission is to help protect butterfly habitat. The organization gets its name from the Xerces blue, a butterfly driven to extinction in California in 1943.

Tropical Forests

Many types of forest grow in tropical America, Africa, Asia, and Australia, but the ones we hear most about are rain forests. Tropical rain forests are filled with sounds, colors, sudden movements, and lush vegetation. More creatures live here than in any other forest on Earth. One tree alone can be home to more than a thousand kinds of insects—not just a thousand individuals, but a thousand species of beetle, ant, butterfly, bee, and many more!

Rain forests of these tropical regions are as varied as the kinds of animals that live in the branches, leaves, and roots of the trees themselves. Rain forests in their many forms occur only where moisture is abundant. The rainiest rain forest, for example, is on the island of Kauai in Hawaii, where the average rainfall is 40 feet each year. That's 40 inches per month—more rain than falls in an entire year in the city of Seattle, Washington, a place known for its gray skies and soggy climate!

But tropical forests can also be dry, very dry. Just as in the United States, the rainfall and other conditions that affect forest growth vary greatly from place to place, and within any tropical country, the rain forest gives way to dry forests that are actually the most threatened of all the major tropical forests in the world. According to one of the most knowledgeable tropical scientists, Dr. Daniel Janzen, there were about 550,000 square kilometers of dry forest (an area about the size of all of France) along the Pacific coast of Central and South America when Europeans first settled shortly after Columbus arrived. Today only about 480 square kilometers of that forest are protected. So little remains outside national parks and other refuge areas that we must grow new dry forests to get an idea of what these woodlands are really like.

There are many reasons to save both the dry forests and the rain forests of the tropics. Species living in the rain forest's lush vegetation reach such great numbers and come in so many kinds that scientists discover new plant and animal species almost every day. It's as if the rain forest decided to hold a contest to find out how many ways to feather a bird, put legs on an insect, or stick branches on a tree. Rain-forest flowers seem to hold a beauty pageant all their own—their colors and fragrances are so dazzling and so incredibly varied. But the diversity of tropical woodlands can unravel almost as rapidly as we discover the new species living within them.

Rain-forest life is incredibly fragile for many of the same reasons it is so incredibly wonderful. Tropical woodlands can lose species quickly when just a small amount of forest is cleared, because more species are packed into every square inch than they are in North American forests. Many of those species are *endemics*—species that live only in one particular

TROPICAL FOREST SOILS

Soils on the floors of tropical forests are thin, unlike the much deeper and richer soils of our northern forests. Once trees are removed, the loss of what little soil exists results in devastation of nutrients in the ground. Soil is simply washed away by the pounding rains. Small groups of native peoples working the land used to clear small areas of tropical forest, grow some crops, then move on to a new area. Since their clearings were small, this use of the land did not harm the forest over time.

Now far larger farms and ranches have spread into the forest. In Brazil these agricultural areas are known as fazendas, huge business ranches that cover hundreds or thousands of acres.

Cattle are grazed on cleared land, but the land is not able to sustain the grazing pressure, and new forests are cleared in an ongoing effort by those who value the tropical forests only as a place to grow beef.

Brazil is trying to stop forest destruction, in part through a plan outlined in 1989 and known as "Nossa Natureza" (Our Nature). A set of 17 presidential decrees, the plan ends former government encouragement for cattle ranching in forested areas and creates a special police force to help control forest destruction.

If you would like to know more people who live in rain forests, contact the Fundacao Nacional do Indio, Assessoria de Comunicacao Social, SIA Trecho 04, Lote 750, Brasília DF, CEP 71200 Brazil. As in North America, native people have lived in harmony with forest-land for thousands of years. How have they been able to live without destroying the woodlands? Perhaps there are lessons to be learned from the people who still live within Brazilian forests, such as the protected national park-lands so different from our own — parks where people are a part of nature.

Also, read books about people of the forest, including these:
PEOPLE OF THE TROPICAL RAINFOREST by Denslow and Padoch.
AMAZON by Kelly and London.
DREAMS OF AMAZONIA by Stone.
AMAZON TOWN: A STUDY OF MAN IN THE TROPICS by Wagley.

NUSAGANDI PARK

A park that grew from concern by young people about their forests and homeland, Nusagandi is a protected area that contains untouched tropical forest (referred to as neg serret) along the coast of Panama. Kuna young people of Panama became concerned about nonnative encroachment and eventually received support from scientists to help them establish Nusagandi Park. The reserve that has been created by Kuna such as Guillermo Archibald stands in sharp contrast to the surrounding lands that are being cleared at alarming rates. In Panama more than 120,000 acres of tropical forest are lost each year. The Kuna wish this land to be left in its wild, forested condition as they always have left it. To the Kuna, the People's Place and nature are not separate areas. They know the forest sustains their life, offering medicinal plants, as well as food and other intangible rewards.

Within Nusagandi Park, scientists have discovered 15 new plant species already — species never known to people other than Kunas. They have also identified 80 endangered plants and animals that are now finding a safe refuge within a park because young Kuna people cared enough to protect their own special forest.

---

place. Ecuador offers us a good, though sad, example of what this means. In its western regions, Ecuador was once home to about 8,000 to 10,000 plant species and an estimated 200,000 or more kinds of animals.

Since 1960, more than 90 percent of the Ecuadoran forests have been cleared to make room for banana farms and human settlement, and to explore for oil. As a result of the forest destruction, scientists believe the world has lost as many as 50,000 plant and animal species in just this one South American country.

Tropical forests are home to at least two of every three living plants and animals on Earth. Some scientists estimate that there are 3 million species living there. Others say there are as many as 100 million. No one knows for sure. And most of those species don't even have names yet. At the current rate of forest loss, we can expect to say good-bye forever to half of them during the next 20 years.

If things don't change, five plant species will become extinct every day from now until the turn of the century. That's a total of 50,000 species—10 times the number of kinds of trees, flowers, shrubs, and grasses in all of eastern North America! Some of the species we will lose could cure diseases or become new and valuable food sources. More important, much of the tropical forestland is already home to people who have lived and worked within these woodlands for centuries. They are people who can probably teach us how they have borrowed from the forest without destroying it for all those years. As a student recently commented, perhaps the simplest way to save the forest is to listen to those who live there; her suggestion was to learn the languages of the peoples south of our borders.

This idea comes at a time when forest burning is increasing the carbon dioxide levels, which many people believe causes the greenhouse effect. This is a global problem requiring our understanding and increased communication with each other, since we all have so much to lose or to gain from our actions in the next decade.

So use the information you do have wisely, and search for more ways to awaken people to your concerns about wildlife. Others just might get excited enough to help you, especially if you tell them that, according to the U.S. Office of Technology Assessment, we lose a chunk of tropical forest that is as big as the entire state of California every two years.

Together you might embrace the needs of tropical animals such as the 200 worldwide members of the primate families that include the lemurs, tarsiers, chimpanzees, howler monkeys, and gorillas. You might adopt the needs of parrots, toucans, quetzels, macaws, iiwis, sunbirds, or tropical hummingbirds. But remember our own North American past, too! North America is home to many migrating birds, such as the

TROPICAL RAIN FORESTS OF THE WORLD

Countries with the greatest amount of rain forest include: Brazil, Indonesia, Zaire, Peru, India, Colombia, Mexico, Bolivia, Papua New Guinea, Burma, Venezuela, Congo, Malaysia, Gabon, Guyana, Cameroon, Surinam, Ecuador, and Madagascar. Tropical rain forests in the United States exist only in the Hawaiian Islands, where nearly half of the largest remaining lowland rain forest dominated by native species was destroyed during 1984 and 1985 in an attempt to generate electricity from wood chips.

warblers that visit northern forests in summer, then fly south when winter arrives. These migrating animals lead an international life looking for seasonal homes. Choose animals like these to lead you into an exploration of forests in other lands. Or search for the way that feels right for you, remembering that many friends await your help, young and old alike. To get in touch with kids in Central America, Asia, or Africa to share your ideas about saving forests, contact others who have already done the same. Various groups have started rain-forest projects such as the Costa Rican Bosque Eterno de los Ninos (Children's Rain Forest). This effort encourages local protection of the forest through careful management of existing forest, reforestation, and expansion of valuable refuge areas. Write to the MONTEVERDE CONSERVATION LEAGUE, Apartado 10165-1000, San José, Costa Rica, for more information about this model project.

When you close this book, walk into a forest or woodland near your home and look around. Listen. Smell the change of seasons, and feel the air moving through the branches. We now know that this is not simply a place to enjoy, nor is it a place to thoughtlessly destroy, as in times past. This is a place to save in new ways. Choose one. Follow where it leads. Just get out there and do it.

TROPICAL FORESTS

WHERE TO WRITE

Organizations that help tropical forests of the Americas include the following:

National Audubon Society, 950 Third Avenue, New York, NY 10022

World Wildlife Fund, 1250 24th Street NW, Washington, DC 20037

Rainforest Action Network, 300 Broadway, Suite 28, San Francisco, CA 94133

The Basic Foundation, P.O. Box 47012, St. Petersburg, Florida 33743

Rainforest Alliance, 295 Madison Avenue, Suite 1804, New York, NY 10017

Fundacao Pro Natureza (FUNATURA), Latin American Program, 1785 Massachusetts Avenue NW, Washington, DC 20036

Environmental Defense Fund, 257 Park Avenue South, New York, NY 10010

Conservation International, 1015 18th Street NW, Suite 1002, Washington, DC 20036

Afterword

Kids across the country have been planting trees, building birdhouses, and voicing their concerns about forests and forest wildlife. You are the ones who can make a difference. All your actions do help. But your job is not an easy one.

As you have seen in this book, many animals will need your continued help to survive. That will take lots of work and the help of many more people. But don't think that you have to save every forest or each animal. Single out a forest or an endangered face that means a lot to you. Work first to protect an area you know about or one that is close to home.

Try also to join with other people nearby and far from your home. Spread your own ideas and share projects with others. Right now there are so very few people with full-time jobs to protect the environment that your volunteer help is highly valuable. The National Audubon Society and other organizations welcome your help. Join them, and we can all work together to make sure the world is always home to grizzly bears, eagles, and the dazzling little warblers that brighten our forests from coast to coast.

Choose some forest-saving actions, and the world will be much better for what you have done. In your hands, our One Earth will be a better home for all life to share.

ONE EARTH

Index